The Contented Classroom
Strategies for Teacher Happiness

Written by
Arlene Prewitt

Illustrated by
Susan Kropa

Cover by
Jeff Van Kanegan

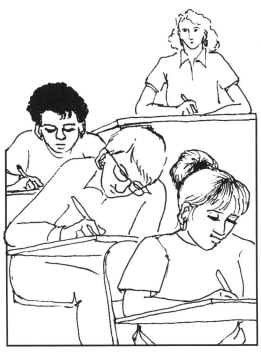

Publisher
Instructional Fair • TS Denison
Grand Rapids, MI 49544

ISBN: 0-7424-0125-1
The Contented Classroom
Copyright © 2001 Instructional Fair • TS Denison
a Division of Instructional Fair Group, Inc.
3195 Wilson Dr. NW
Grand Rapids, Michigan 49544

introduction

Many times in my role as a teacher, I experienced frustration, discouragement, and unhappiness. I thought that something was wrong with me, and my confidence as a teacher was so low that I would at times avoid contact with other teachers. In department meetings, the "stars" of the group would speak up about their students who had achieved awesome awards, or they would fascinate us with some new project that their students were enthusiastically pursuing that was sure to get headlines! In these meetings, I remained quiet and assumed an interested air. Inside, I was thinking, "I will never be a good teacher."

After years of exposure, I came to the conclusion that I am indeed a "good" teacher. Sometimes the "stars" are just more verbal and expressive. I did some classroom visitations and learned that their good ideas could be transmitted to my classroom. I became confident enough to share my ideas one-on-one and to take other teachers' ideas for my own use. As a result, my intimidation began to evaporate.

Still, I was not really happy in the classroom. I read some literature on happiness and one day I said to myself, "Arlene, if you aren't happy in the classroom, where do you plan to be happy? You spend a lot of time here." Not only did I talk to myself, but I listened; and that day I made a vow that I would use every legitimate means available to find happiness in the classroom. That one simple decision changed my life.

Once I began to see my colleagues realistically, I realized that I was not alone. One of the "stars" confided that there were days when she wished she could just "walk off the job." A passion was born inside me to help other teachers who struggled in the classroom and consumed their precious time at home sharing their frustration and unhappiness. If the principles that I found and employed to create a fulfilled and happy existence in the classroom could be shared, perhaps other teachers could adapt the strategies into their own lives.

You will find this book full of my experiences and observations of the experiences of others. It is my hope that as you read you will have moments of inspiration that will influence your attitudes and actions in a positive manner. If we are not happy in our jobs, we are losing a precious amount of time that can never be retrieved. On the other hand, those who adopt the attitudes and employ the simple exercises that bring contentment will gain satisfaction and fulfillment that will affect every area of life.

Table of Contents

CHAPTER 1

Happiness is a Decision

Imagine the average conference-going, motivation-seeking person, sitting comfortably in an auditorium, waiting for the words of wisdom to fall from the lips of a highly paid conference speaker; and without warning the body of this hungry spirit is jarred from the seat with a statement such as, "Happiness is a decision." Having heard that statement coming from the mouth of a speaker who had been commissioned to give a motivational speech, I skeptically thought, "I'm not happy, but I didn't decide to be unhappy. What a ridiculous thought!" I leaned back in my seat and looked around at the other participants, but they all seemed to have that "go ahead and give it to me, Baby" look. Looking back at the speaker, it was all I could do to maintain a civil expression on my face. The smile and smug look of the speaker, who obviously had made the "choice" to be happy, made me furious.

It was now evident that I was in need of more motivation, so my husband coerced me to go with him to another conference. The speaker must have graduated from the same school of persuasion as the previous speaker. After making the usual introductory jokes, he looked out into the audience, pointed a long index finger, and declared firmly, "You are exactly where you want to be in life." This statement filled me with indignation and resentment. It seemed terribly presumptuous on the part of a speaker to assume knowledge of the audience and make blanket statements in regard to our life situations. Actually, I wasn't where I wanted to be at that moment! My sitting in that auditorium was a result of my husband's strong suggestion to attend the meeting along with him. Where I wanted to be in life was a whole different matter!

Over the next few days, those words, "You are exactly where you want to be," kept echoing in my mind, and I mentioned the incident to a former student of mine, who had invited me to join him for lunch in the student union at the college where I was then teaching. Since I was the teacher and he was the student, I expected some kind of sympathetic agreement. To my surprise, without hesitation, the student said, "I absolutely agree." Feeling betrayed, I explored a little further. "How can I be exactly where I want to be when the choices are made by my husband, and, in my background and culture, following him is expected?"

The young man looked me straight in the eye and said, "Your choices have brought you to where you are now. You could have chosen not to come along. You could leave your husband today and have your own career in any city that you choose. Nobody is making you do anything. You are a product of your choices." Wow! Let that soak in gradually! After examining that statement, the truth of it became evident. In fact, I was so impressed with the exercising of such an act of will on my part that a good feeling began to surface in regard to my position in life. It was true that I could have redirected my life at any crossroads of the past. Of course, my decisions had been affected by traditions, training, and family expectations, but no one had forced me into compliance, and I could change directions any day. The new perception changed my concept from the image of victim to that of commander. The new image brought me a peace and happiness toward myself and toward the position that I had "chosen" to follow.

Some time later in an after-school class designed to help students make up a credit, a confirmation that our destiny comes as a result of our choices came as a response to one high school student who complained to the class in general about the difficulty involved in meeting all the graduation requirements. A senior attempted to encourage the weary scholar by reminding her, "Life is one percent choice and ninety-nine percent consequences." Whether it helped the disgruntled student or not was never documented, but the statement sank into my memory bank. After digesting that bit of wisdom and applying it to my discontent, I realized that my earlier unhappy complaints had been with consequences because I had denied my part in the choices. The acceptance of myself as a woman who made choices added a powerful dimension of happiness.

Having wasted several years feeling sorry for myself and nursing unhappiness, the decision to change was a welcome hope. Hoping to find the secret of happiness by doing some research, I began to look for happy people, those who were really happy, not the ones who just had highs and lows. If I could discover what brought them happiness, maybe their secret could be integrated into my life and into the lives of others around me. Most people have moments of happiness, but maintaining a happy state of mind seems difficult. I wanted happiness to take up residence, to be a permanent fixture, to become a way of life.

As the intrigue with the idea of happiness in regard to productivity increased, there was created a definite sharpening of sensitivity and awareness in the observation of others. One evening while traveling in Europe, another teacher and I were sitting in an outdoor section of a depot in Paris, France, waiting for a train which would take us to Pisa, Italy. I gradually became aware of a very unpleasant, unidentifiable odor that quickly grew more pronounced. Looking around for clues, I noticed a very large, unkempt woman approaching. She was asking for money. She passed through the row in front of me, and accompanying her approach was the worst smell that I have ever encountered emanating from a human being. Her body was layered in rolls of flesh; her hair was thickly matted; her face was bloated; her shapeless dress, slick with dirt, was hanging loosely to her ankles in uneven folds; her shoes, flapping when she walked, were huge, loosely-fitting, adapted men's work shoes with no strings, and slits had been cut allowing the little toes to protrude. Even her high-pitched, demanding voice had a grating, irritating quality as she asked for coins. If I could paint a picture of an unhappy woman, this pitiful specimen would have matched my idea for a model. Nothing, not one characteristic about her, was pleasant or desirable.

After she departed the immediate area, the smell lingered for some time, but while watching the parade of everyday life in the station, I forgot her. In a few minutes, the odor began to drift again in my direction but not as pronounced as before. Turning my head in curiosity, I was rewarded with a picture of sublime happiness. The beggar was sitting a few rows back and was blissfully eating a sandwich purchased from a vender in the station. I doubt if I have ever looked that happy while eating prime rib at my favorite steak house! She ate noisily, licking her fingers all the while. The beggar was obviously relishing every bite as she sat quietly and dined, oblivious to all around her. The expression even on that bloated and dirty face had changed to one of accomplishment and delight. I could now paint that picture (if I were endowed with such a talent), using the same model, and call it "Happiness."

Another example of the hypothesis that happiness does not depend on one's financial circumstance was illustrated through a former sophomore in my regular English II class. Allison reported to class clean and neatly dressed in clothing that was faddish at the time. Her appearance signaled that she shopped at cheaper stores than some of her classmates, but her charm and beauty made up for what might have been missing in dollars.

Allison exemplified academic conscientiousness and had earned an A for the quarter until I made a request for notebooks to be submitted for the last grade of the quarter. After recording the grades, I noticed that Allison's name was followed by a blank space in the notebook column of the grade book. The next day, I reminded her that the notebook was due and that her grade had slid to a B without the notebook. She quietly replied, "I know," and she offered no excuse. I stood speechless because she had never failed to turn in an assignment, and I knew that she had all the notebook requirements in her bookbag.

Why had she not assembled it into the designated sections and submitted it for grading? My curiosity would not allow the incident to pass without a second try. The next morning, I called her back to my desk and again asked, "Allison, aren't you going to turn in your notebook?"

I don't think I will ever forget her reply. "Mrs. Prewitt," she began, "nobody buys me anything. I work at McDonalds and buy everything that I have. I have to pay rent to my family, buy my own clothes, buy my food, and pay any educational fees I may have. So, if I can leave it off, I don't buy it. I never bought a notebook." She said all of this with a quiet smile and a cheerfulness as though she were reassuring me that my concern was unfounded. She had a list of priorities, and a notebook was low on the list. She had made a decision that she could live with, even happily it seemed. Needless to say, the next day several extra notebooks mysteriously appeared in my room for the taking. No other exchange in regard to notebooks was made, but it made me happy when I saw one of the notebooks on her desk. From that day on, I have never required an item of a student without making extras available.

At another motivational conference (targeting possibility-thinking women), a keynote speaker encouraged the participants to be happy and gave ways in which to bring happiness into our lives. I took notes because at the time I felt that my life exemplified high-level stress and unfulfilled dreams and that happiness was probably one of those momentary or elusive dreams that could only be experienced in childhood. In way of a strategy, the speaker suggested that we literally set a trash can by our bed at night and go through a cleansing-of-the-mind procedure. This exercise consisted of lifting our hand to our head, making believe we were pulling the offending thought from our brain, and then moving our hand over to the waiting trash can and opening the hand to turn loose of the unpleasant mental invader. I agree that happiness begins with an emptying out rather than a taking in, but a mere physical exercise may not be the answer. Consider the world of technology for an illustration of the emptying-out process.

A little knowledge of the Macintosh computer will give an analogy for the mental garbage dumping exercise. The Macintosh computer has a trash can which looks much like the ones that line the streets on garbage pickup day. All documents filed in the hard drive of the computer or on the disk are listed in the files. If the user wants to clean out the files, the unnecessary document (garbage) is specified and dragged (the screen actually pictures this process) over to the little trash can at the bottom of the screen. When the garbage reaches the trash can, the operator releases the button which drops the garbage into the trash can. We now have a duplication of the trash-dumping process, a type of virtual reality approach, that was suggested by the conference speaker.

For the visual learner, perhaps the lesson of the computer will accent the process of emptying the garbage from a memory file, and we will be able to apply that principle to our mental and emotional systems to rid ourselves of accumulated, unwanted garbage. The initial step is to recognize that we have stored garbage before we can start the cleansing process. We may find it surprising when we uncover all the garbage that can accumulate in the mind, spirit, and emotions. Garbage is sometimes hidden or even treasured as an item to keep. The act of letting go may seem to be a concession that we were somehow in the wrong. If someone has wronged us, the hurt may be pleasant, a validation that we are in the right. Nonetheless, many of our stored ideas and memories of past behavior can be blocking the passageway to happiness.

After a person has deliberately made the decision to be happy, disturbing circumstances (exempting extreme cases) become bumps in the road of life. On one of the episodes of the sitcom *Frazier*, all the characters spent the evening in self-inventory because an animal psychiatrist had told them that Eddie, the dog, was sad and not eating because someone close to him was transferring unhappiness. After the evening of misery in which each character took the blame because each had allowed an unhappy situation to fester in the emotional bank, Eddie suddenly, miraculously recovered after finding his missing Barbie® doll. Frazier's brilliant lesson to be learned was, "Life is too short to dwell on every bump in the road." How many times have we observed an associate who has become unproductive and cannot seem to move on because some trivial (as we see it) matter has stolen his or her thunder? We want to use the buzz words, "Get over it!" or "Get a life!" These bumps may slow down progress, we may have to stop and change our course, but the active decision to be happy has become a part of our defense mechanism, and we will find the courage to overcome the obstacles.

Suggestions for Making the Decision to Be Happy

1. Recognition of the need for a decision to be happy is foremost. Sometimes we may accept our unhappy condition as perfectly normal. We compare ourselves to a neighbor down the hall who moans a lot more than we do. Do we, indeed, want to be unhappy at all? Are we settling for less and deciding to live lives of "quiet desperation"?

2. After the decision is made, do some mental exercises (use the mental garbage can or picture the computer dumping station) to release the negative thoughts that have accumulated in your mental storage bins. Be creative and make it your personal method. Some of the garbage is so deeply hidden from the conscious mind that you may think it is forgotten. Injustices and hurts as old as childhood may still be stored in an obscure bin. This process may take some time because the items contaminating happiness will not all surface at once. The "delete all" key for your brain and emotional system does not exist. Use today to work with one piece of garbage. Once you have started identifying your personal garbage and letting it go, the process will become familiar and your progress will be measurable.

3. Feel proud of the slightest success. You have embarked on a journey whose destination may seem at an unreachable distance. At this point you may venture only a small step, but you can celebrate the launching. Recently, I received an e-mail that ended with this tag: "Happiness is a journey, not a destination."

4. Refrain from comparing your state of happiness to that of someone who is wallowing in misery. If you need a role model, explore the thinking and mind sets of someone who seems to be happy. Do some research to increase your sensitivity. Actually, people do not mind the question, "How can you always be happy or cheerful?"

CHAPTER 2

Developing Career Pride

We have all heard the teaching profession referred to as the last entry in a vocational choice list, especially under the designation of "professional opportunities." Soon after high school graduation, I dated a teacher who apologized for his career choice by quoting the phrase, "If you can't do anything else, then teach." Teacher salaries usually reflect the low end of the professional career spectrum, especially in the beginning years. Low salaries may be a factor in lowering our pride, and, as a result, we may feel less respected than those who have chosen more lucrative fields. I once heard a teacher say, "If those business teachers (or computer teachers) are so good, why aren't they out there making the big bucks?" But contrary to what those who coin those little sayings may believe, there is that desire to teach, to impart our learning experiences, and to be someone who will make a difference in the lives of the students under our care.

In June of 1999 I, along with three other teachers, took students to Europe. While digging through a bookstore in Oxford, England, I purchased a tiny book of quotations titled *The Best Teacher*. It included many uplifting words of wisdom and humor, but suddenly, in print, I was confronted with the quotation by George Bernard Shaw, "He who can does. He who can't, teaches." I was stunned! I wanted to stand on a soapbox and cry out, "And if 'he can,' who taught him to be able to do? Has 'he' got the guts to stand up before a group of students to mold, teach, mentor, monitor, and care about each individual student's development for one year?" The insult stung, so I tried to reread the quotation searching for various inflections of meaning, trying to find a positive note. The book was ruined!

Who has made the biggest contribution, the doer or the teacher? Perhaps it is a joint contribution. Many highly productive people have given credit to that one teacher in the educational experience who gave encouragement and motivation. Most teachers can document letters or phone calls from students who just wanted to let them know how their lives had been positively influenced through their teacher-student relationship.

Just a few days ago, there was a message on my answering machine at home from a former student. The female voice hesitantly explained, "This is Susan Parker. I'm looking for Mrs. Prewitt who is a teacher. You probably won't remember me, but I had you in English three years ago. Please call if this is you," and she left a long-distance number.

Immediately, I remembered the young lady. She had struggled academically as she actively fought with alcohol addiction at the age of 17. She had been moved back and forth from Mom to Dad with occasional residence in rehabilitation centers in between. While she was in my class, she became pregnant, and I was the first adult with whom she confided this awesome news. What a responsibility for me, just a teacher in her life, to be someone that she considered trustworthy enough to share the most intimate thoughts of her sad life. Her major fear was that her father would "kick" her out and she would have nowhere to go since the father of the child had mysteriously disappeared from the scene. Susan started missing classes and finally withdrew to enter yet another rehabilitation center. She later visited my classroom to tell me she was better and had decided to keep the baby, but she could not see her way clear to enroll in classes. Chances were that I would never see her again even though she promised she would stay in touch.

Of course, I called Susan that very evening. From many miles away she happily replied, "Mrs. Prewitt, I'm so glad you called. I just wanted you to know that I have been sober for two years." She went on, "After my little girl was born, I knew that I had to get my life together to be a good mother. I am now married to a wonderful man, and he wants me to go back to school." She continued, "I wanted to let you know that you were so wonderful to care about me that I want to go into some type of teaching, maybe a teacher's aide. I would like to help someone else."

Do you think I went to bed that night thinking, "He who can't, teaches"? No! I went to bed content with being at the top of the success ladder. Of course, that success will never show on a salary chart or a chart of any kind, but there is nothing comparable for job fulfillment. I don't need a bumper sticker or a special badge that declares, "I make a difference." I know it; I can document it; therefore, no one can belittle my choice of profession.

Pride in our career choice of teacher may come gradually. Our first few years in the classroom can be difficult and create grounds for questioning our choice. Last spring, Walter, a young teacher in his second year, came to my room to air a grievance involving the dismissal of another teacher. He wasn't looking for a solution; he just needed to tell someone how he felt about what he considered to be an injustice on the part of the administration. In fact, he felt a little guilty because he had worked with the other teacher and felt himself to be a silent participant in the alleged injustice. Walter felt totally helpless; but, not being able to let it rest, he crusaded on behalf of the other teacher who was being released for what Walter perceived as unjust cause.

For some reason, it seems that educators are to be the all-good, all-understanding, all-caring, halo-wearing segment of society. Stories of the early American educators promote the idea of teachers being cast in the above-human idyllic roles. Therefore, when the educator is exposed as a normal human being doing his/her job, the results can be devastating. Walter's dream bubble of the ideal educational world had taken its final blow and had collapsed, leaving him devastated. As I listened to him pour out his story, both sides of the conflict became easily visible, but he could see just one side. I thought, "What should I do? Do I try to get a pump and blow him another bubble? Do I justify the alleged wrong and try to make it a right? Do I just pat his hand and cry with him?"

As he summarized his unhappiness, he confided, "If this is how education is going to be, I'm not sure I want to be a part of it. I've been thinking of looking elsewhere for another career." Walter is at the point of making a decision which will result in more crossroads. His disillusionment has resulted in his wondering if he still wants to be a teacher since the educational world has not turned out to be the nurturing setting that he had read about in his college textbooks. He feels wronged, and his inability to help his colleague makes him feel helpless. Never has education looked more like an institution. Even the union could not restore his colleague's position, which adds to Walter's feelings of defenselessness.

Walter is young; he has invested two years. He can either give up and live in disillusionment with the education world, or he can say goodbye to the colleague and decide to make the best of the career he has chosen and for which he has prepared. If he chooses to remain in education, he must empty the garbage and cleanse himself of the feelings associated with the alleged injustice. He will not be happy as a teacher while nursing the wounds. They will only grow and eventually permeate his attitudes and his effectiveness in the classroom.

Ordinarily, rather than give advice, I just let the unhappy person vent the frustrations, but in this case, I told Walter that he had two choices. "If you stay with education, you must let the incident go. Get over it! Accept the fact that you just may not have all the details. If you can't get over it, then you will begin to get bitter and neither you, your coworkers, or your students will find the atmosphere of your classroom pleasant. On the other hand, if you are going to remain defensive and unhappy, then go look for that other career." He is back this fall and I haven't heard any more about the issue. He has a big smile when I pass him in the hallway. Walter has obviously chosen to move on and be happy.

What about that teacher who is not as fortunate as Walter in that he or she has already invested 15 to 20 years into the profession? That teacher may be blind to the fact that storing every small (or big) action of injustice or hurt will accumulate in the mental and emotional systems and spread like a cancer. As a result, the teacher may experience an emotional state much like that of physical entrapment. Unless that teacher takes a positive step in the direction of releasing those wounds, the career becomes a sentence and the system becomes the prison. As the spirit of an unhappy teacher is saturated with discontent and discouragement, visible indicators will surface. Fault-finding becomes a pastime. Nothing is ever right. The cafeteria food is nasty, the cafeteria help is unfriendly, the administration is moronic, the teachers are cliquish, the students are idiots, and the list goes on.

The movie, *Mr. Holland's Opus*, gives a clear picture of different stages of a teacher's attitude and performance. Mr. Holland evolved from a mercenary who ran to beat the buses from the parking lot, to a man who gave of himself to see students accomplish even a small portion of success. The teacher who senses the drum beat of the school and marches in step will find interests past the 3:00 dismissal. Those marching out of step will find the road much more difficult. Also, the tendency to criticize our colleagues increases when we are not in the rhythm of the whole group. Once we give in to that temptation to participate in a conversation of put-downs or questions in regard to our colleagues' actions, the seed has been sown for future sessions, and we may find ourselves marching to the beat of discontentment and unhappiness.

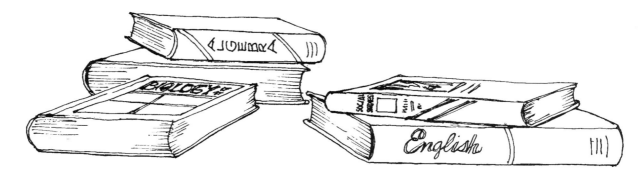

Why is it that the people who appear most happy in a school are likely those who are most involved? Granted, they will inform us from time to time of their overtime input, but they are busy assisting in student activities. Benjamin Franklin suggested that "an idle mind is the Devil's workshop." By experience, I know that the busier I am, the less time I have for pity parties. After working four hours extra one day, I went home feeling exhilarated because a team of teachers had put together a project. Even though we had spent extra time with no extra pay, the camaraderie and team effort left a pleasant feeling. The next morning I greeted the assistant principal who had worked with us, and my immediate comment was, "I feel great about the work we did yesterday." His smile was accompanied by, "Me, too. All of you should feel as though you have accomplished a lot!" Wow! If I had gone home at 3:00, I would have missed the chance to work on a team and to enjoy the afterglow of accomplishment.

On the other hand, I have tangled a few times with that monster of discouragement. A few years back, there was a time in my teaching that I became discouraged with my personal progress and that of my students. I tended to withdraw from other teachers rather than seek help. My lack of interest even manifested itself in my clothing choices. My selections reflected an "I don't care how I look" attitude. In the mornings, I would think, "I'll just be in my classroom all day and won't see anyone, so it doesn't matter what I wear." That attitude began to affect other areas of my life. Failure to look inward for the root of my distress prolonged the realization that it was up to me to find the antidote. It wasn't long until I realized that I did not like my new image. Whoever coined that phrase, "Today is the first day of the rest of your life!" has done more good than he or she will ever realize. It reinforces the truth that we always have the opportunity and choice to begin again, to start over.

Of course, during that time period I saw the students as nonproductive entities, wandering in the maze of institutionalism. Critical attitudes point fingers and give indication that the critic is experiencing some type of superiority disillusionment. I even wrote a poem to express my disillusionment and proudly submitted it for publication. I hope no one read it (probably didn't since it was published in a large volume of amateur poets seeking an audience) or took it seriously because it sent a message that I do not subscribe to today. However, I will share the poem to illustrate the state of mind that permeated my being.

The Classroom

Faces in a void—
waiting
in blank, listlessness,
devoid of response;
Blank Tablets, isolated in a vacuum;

Drone of monologue,
flat-lining the pulses
lodged in uninhabited flesh
of Ducklike resistance;

Figures in trances,
fixed in hollow orbit
of perpetual motion
meeting no obstacle.

Who will send flowers?
Who will shed tears?
Who will recite the eulogy?
Who will record the passing?

Proudly, I made copies of this poem and shared it with my students (English II and III regular) at the end of the poetry unit. First of all, they had no idea who had died! After explaining that the first stanza described the students, the second stanza described the teacher's effect on the students, the third stanza reflected the students' daily activities, and the fourth one was mourning the death of education, they were still unimpressed.

Undaunted, and being proud of my poetry skills, I analyzed the poem line by line. Of course, they had never heard of John Locke and his "blank tablet" application to the pure mind of the baby where experience is recorded. They failed to be ecstatic over the metaphor which compared the teacher delivering lessons which rolled over them (the students) like water poured on a duck in "ducklike resistance." One student displayed a look of discovery and reported, "Oh, now I get it. The orbit is the route we take from classroom to classroom!" I began to quiver with excitement at this breakthrough. I became impassioned with my poem (notice that I did not say with my students or with my subject matter). I was ranking right up there with T. S. Eliot's "hollow men." As I saw it at the time, we were all hollow!

Encouraged in my analysis of the educational system, I shared the poem with my English Composition 1102 class at the college where I served as an adjunct. They jumped on it enthusiastically, analyzing, commenting, asking questions. They all loyally pronounced it as a very good poem and one that should be published. I had been validated! However, one student remained after class and with an almost injured tone in his voice asked, "Mrs. Prewitt, is that the way you really feel about education, about us as students, and about yourself as a teacher?" I replied, "It's just a poem. You know how literature goes to the extremes to make us see a balance. Writers use personas." I hope the answer was sufficient to reassure him that we weren't all going into oblivion.

What that student said had an effect on me. I began to look at my attitudes and assess the message that was being given in the classroom. I decided that I didn't feel the way that I had written, and the thrill of the subject and the power of embellishment had triggered the fatal outcome. The poem had already been published, so no retraction was possible. At the time of writing, I was expressing my state of mind about education, not the reality. Perhaps that one student's comments helped pave the way to the self-realization that I not only wanted to change my attitude but that I wanted to be happy. Had I not consciously made a decision to be happy, I may still be wandering in the maze of disillusionment, never discovering the joy of teaching.

At times, a teacher will express discouragement in the salary schedule and compare salaries made by other members of the family or friends in challenging and interesting jobs. Restless and unhappy teachers may have tried some of the get-rich-quick schemes and may have ended up spending more money than they made. There may be a time when a teacher must weigh all the options and admit that he or she really likes teaching and would choose this career all over again. With this decision, the teacher is ready to begin the journey to self-fulfillment, which will result in a more contented atmosphere within the classroom.

Teachers are constantly encouraged in staff development meetings to become involved in innovative methods of teaching. On the other hand, there are always those few on the faculty who feel that their classroom techniques have worked well for years and should for many more. They continue to hand out the time-yellowed papers to students. This type of rut can result in poor performance and a disgruntled attitude. New ideas become a threat to the status quo and may be met with immediate defense mechanisms.

Our attitude toward our career will affect our teaching and our students. I have had students ask me if I felt underpaid. I usually answer, "No." They share that they have heard teachers complain in the classroom of their pay, unfair treatment, or some other unhappiness. Our happiness or unhappiness will be communicated to our associates and may have an influence on our credibility and effectiveness in classroom administration.

One great example of career pride can be found in the person of Colonel Harland Sanders of Kentucky Fried Chicken® fame. Colonel Sanders had a small restaurant and court (little cottages) in my hometown of Corbin, Kentucky. As a small child, I became aware of his presence through his amazing appearance. The Colonel was operating a small business in a little town of 6,000 or less, but he treated his business and his customers as though they were participating in a classic experience. He always dressed in the now-famous white suit with the string tie, and he drove a long, white Cadillac. The white hair, mustache, goatee, and cane were part of him—not just a promotional gimmick. My first remembrance of Colonel Sanders was watching him get into his car. I had never seen a man in a white suit or a white Cadillac. As a child, I thought that this beautiful man was a very important person. He had pride that made those around him very aware that he considered his business and his customers to be important enough to wear his very best. Likewise, we as teachers may feel that our audience and influence is extremely limited, but for our own well-being, we must remind ourselves that we are not just feeding a stomach—we are feeding a mind and spirit whose influence will reach far beyond the door of the classroom. We may never drive a white Cadillac or its equivalent, but we can step with pride. Our influence is perpetual.

To expect any teacher to make an immediate change and become a zestful proponent of the classroom activities would be stretching it a bit. But in time, if that teacher can be encouraged to find a new academic interest, then career excitement can be rekindled. Teaching will no longer seem a mere dispensation of information, but the teacher will become an instrument in the changing and challenging process of educating a child.

The decision to make a positive change must be followed with actions that lead to that change. The crossover is not automatic. Most of us have likely spent some time in that vacuum portrayed so well in *Mr. Holland's Opus*, where we have lost some of our early dreams and have failed to replace them with dreams that can be actualized within the framework of our exposure. At times we may find ourselves devitalized to the point of incompetence in the classroom. There is hope. Acknowledging the need is the first step.

Suggestions for Promoting Pride in Teaching as a Profession

1. Recognize the feelings of discouragement and the need for a change of attitude.

2. Find someone in the school who is enthusiastically pursuing a project or teaching activity. Spend some time with that person asking questions about his/her activities related to the project.

3. When someone else is sharing an innovative idea, give your support.

4. Actively seek some new idea (at least new to you) that interests you and get involved.

5. Choose a school team (basketball, etc.) and become an avid fan. A team which involves some of your own students may provide some classroom enthusiasm. If students see you at their activities, they tend to be more supportive of you in the classroom.

6. Find something good and compliment a colleague today.

7. On days that you expect to be difficult, wear your favorite outfit or favorite accessory.

Easing into Reality

When thinking of living two lives, a person might automatically think of the man or woman who is cheating on a spouse or a person who concurrently works two very different jobs. Ironically, these two situations cannot be labeled as reasons to be unhappy because some personality types may thrive on the "forbidden fruit" idea or the super-busy image. The two lives to which I am referring are more elusive because they lurk in areas which can be kept hidden from others and even from ourselves. We can have accumulated garbage that is a product of our perception of the stimuli we receive. After digesting the information presented to us, our emotional and mental reactions can play havoc in our thought processes. To be more specific, we can go through our days oscillating between reality and fantasy.

We perceive and interpret the way we live and then use labels such as satisfactory/unsatisfactory, happy/sad, barren/fruitful, failure/success, etc. We may not do the labeling consciously or be called upon to verbalize or even recognize our internal process of evaluating our feelings. If we think of happiness as a feeling, we will expect it to come and go with our mood swings. If we perceive happiness as a lifestyle or standard equipment, we will expect it to hang around during the rough times to sustain and nurture us.

The person who uses fantasy to escape the unhappiness of everyday life is similar to the person who takes a drug to alleviate the pain momentarily. There will be that release from the mundane existence, but the treatment addresses the symptom and does not produce a cure. The return-to-normal button will have to be pushed at some point, or we may run the risk of being out of touch with reality. On the other hand, a little escape fantasy may be the thing needed to unwind and momentarily crash from accumulated stress. Most faculties will form social groups that meet outside the walls of the school for some rest and relaxation. Friday afternoons at a local Chili's is a favorite spot for a group of teachers in my school. The meeting is advertised to include whosoever needs to unwind from the week's work.

A woman was introduced to me in a social setting, and her associates had told me that I would simply love Sarah because "she reads all the time." They were sure that we would find a rich background for conversation. Sarah displayed reticence in our early acquaintance, so I thought that she was quite shy. After frequent exchanges of clipped conversation, I grew brave enough to ask, "Sarah, what book are you reading now?" She gave me a vague answer. Her daughter bragged to me that her mother read a book an evening. Such a record is truly impressive! The husband complained that "all she ever does is sit and read." Again, I tried to draw her out with a question about her reading and followed up by sharing an excerpt from what I was currently reading. As in the previous effort, the response was a shy smile and silence. After that encounter, I dropped the subject and talked of mundane things, but I had the sense of a mystery. Some time later, the daughter dropped the tidbit that her mother read nothing but Harlequin romance novels! It is no wonder that she had no intention of discussing her reading with me! After all, as an English teacher, I have never had anyone ask me my opinion of a Harlequin romance novel. Perhaps I can safely assume that the majority of us use escape literature through books, magazines, newspapers, TV shows, and movies to give some release from the stress of survival. At times, I will say to my husband, "Let's go to a movie that entertains and doesn't require analysis or afterthought. I just want to sit and laugh for a little while."

Several years ago, I heard Dr. Norman Vincent Peale deliver an address based on his book, *The Power of Positive Thinking*. He was in his eighties at the time, and I was awestricken with the presence and force of this man who had spearheaded the outpouring of possibility thinking literature. Dr. Peale presented the idea that fantasy is a good technique to escape from the pressures and routine of daily existence. The author instructed the reader to imagine and relive a pleasant experience or to invent a pleasurable fantasy, using great detail as to time, place, surroundings, and companions. Having a vivid imagination, I thought, "This may be the very thing for me." There were many things that I wished to do and places that I wanted to visit. Being an avid reader, I could supply the details with book descriptions. After a day of trivial happenings, this great escape brought me a feeling of pleasure. I'm sure that the author meant this exercise to be infrequent and lasting only a few moments, but like the dangers of drugs, this method can be administered in an overdose, resulting in more discontent and unhappiness. Occasional use may be the antidote for a depressed feeling.

A popular, creative hobby that utilizes Dr. Peale's method of journeying into memory is that of scrapbooking. Full stores of scrapbooking paraphernalia have appeared in malls and shopping centers with names like "Memories." Parties lasting from 5:00 p.m. to midnight are frequent for those who are into scrapbooking. The participants sit around with their own picture collections, their own assortment of thematic or periodic albums, and their markers, stickers, and idea books, and they share ideas while they work on the historical moments of their lives. Personally, I would leave more stressed than I arrived, but, for some, the cropping session is the perfect setting for a few hours of stress release.

There are those school architects and administrators who realize the importance of teacher gathering rooms and provide the space for teachers to have some down time during the day. It is my understanding that elementary teachers stay with their children almost all day, even at lunch. If that is true, I'm sure they envy the schedule of the high school teacher who has a planning period and a free lunch time. I have worked in schools that provided an attractive lounge area for teachers to relax and interact, and I've been in schools that had no such plum to offer. I have found that teachers are much happier when they feel that the administration at least recognizes and attempts to provide for their needs. Departments will sometimes go together to create a room and collectively furnish it with castoff things from their homes. These teachers tend to be very proud (and maybe a little possessive) of "their" room.

Another type of fantasy comes within the realm of expectations. The teacher is housed in a classroom for many hours of the day and spends more time with some of the children than even their own parents do. A relationship develops, and over time the teacher's influence is mammoth. At the outset of the teaching career, a classic fantasy of the beginning teacher involves hungry students, reaching out for the acquired knowledge and expertise of the teacher. Of course, we can all relate to the fantasy that looks like this:
7:30—The tardy bell; all students are in their seats.

7:32—Intercom voice requests, "All rise for the pledge." Every student quietly stands, proudly faces the little American flag limply hanging from the bracket over the chalkboard, places the right hand over the heart, and recites passionately and distinctly the Pledge of Allegiance. After a poignant silence, the students seat themselves with respectful decorum.

7:35—Without being prompted, students open their notebooks and books, retrieve paper and pens from bookbags, and eagerly await the day's challenge.

Most of us would love a day in which we say, "Everyone turn your text to page 1067," and all we hear is the sweet rustling of pages . . . no "What page?" . . . no "Which book?". . . no "What did she say?" . . . no "Did she say page 167?". . . and no snoring sounds coming from the back row! Fantasies come from simple acts such as a classroom activity well received to daydreams of being shipwrecked on a desert island. One teacher told me that her mother checked into the hospital one week out of every year just for the enjoyment of being waited on every moment of the day. She actively planned and packed for this adventure much like she was taking a pleasure vacation. Of course, I think that lady could use a lesson in fantasy building to broaden her horizons.

Recently, a new teacher was hired at my school to replace someone who left in the middle of a semester. Obviously, the new teacher had impressed the hiring assistant principal, but that administrator had one concern that she passed to me as his peer teacher. She asked, "Would you please help Mr. Baker to understand that these students are not going to be sitting there, just waiting for him to dispense wonderful words of wisdom?" She continued, "He's rather intellectual, and I think he is expecting them to

hang onto his every word." I laughed, but she was gravely serious in her concern for this teacher's crash into reality. When I talked with him, he showed me some selections of difficult literature that he was copying to read and discuss with his regular English I and II classes. I knew exactly what the administrator meant, but all teachers must learn a few lessons on their own. I made sure that he had some easier material to fall back on, and it wasn't many days until he was aware that he was in over his head with the deep stuff. Very few of us enter the classroom for the first time without bringing our fantasies of teaching along with us. It doesn't take long for us to realize that we are going to have to redefine our goals and run a reality check.

From the evidence of publication, people enjoy writing and reading letters in the Ann Landers' column of the newspaper that are "how we met" letters. Each writer seems to think that his or her story is unique and tops the others. There should be a column in which teachers could send their stories of their first year of teaching. I heard a keynote address by a college professor who was sure that his first year of experience was more horrid and bizarre than anyone else had ever endured, and he spent half of his presentation time amusing us with his story. Of course, that just baited the hook for every other teacher present to remember that first year and all the unusual and even painful experiences (which may be funny now) that worked the magic of laying many of our fantasies to rest.

Before sharing my first-year experiences, I want to admit to you that I am a first-year-teacher dropout. I make no apologies or excuses. My first teaching position was in Owensboro, Kentucky, at Faust Junior High School for the 1969-1970 school year. Faust was considered a type of inner-city school (enough to get partial forgiveness on my college loan) even though Owensboro did not rate the designation of a big city. I had a teaching job! Somewhere in my faulty understanding, I believed that new teachers were given a textbook and were ushered to a room equipped with several student books along with the usual furniture. At the time of hiring, I was not told that I had been hired to work in a pilot program with seven other teachers in what was labeled the Non-Graded Team Approach to teaching the lowest level of the regular students. Non-Graded meant that seventh and eighth graders were mixed together without a grade designation. I was told that I was to give no homework and use no textbooks or supplementary materials. Can you imagine how inadequate I felt at open house when parents wanted to know why their child, who had always had difficulties in school, now had no textbook and no homework? Everything was to be teacher created. I must have skipped that course in my educational pursuits! To enable us to achieve this mammoth task, we were given an extra free period four days a week.

The word *team* meant that we all shared the same students and the same planning period. Our individual work space was housed in a small room that was set up with eight desks sitting side by side and back to back which gave the sense of working in a rectangle. I assume that the room and the schedule had been carefully planned and implemented to facilitate group interaction, but in the one year I was employed in that school, we never once formally or informally addressed the issues of dealing with the students' needs or with curricular needs. Ideally, one period a week was given to counseling with the students, but I do not recall any counseling actually being done.

Since we were piloting a new program, people came from other schools to observe. Our team leader was very good at showing them around and talking about the program; but I, one of his teammates, was unfamiliar with the objectives (if any) or expected outcomes (if any). In fact, after the superintendent hired me, I was sent to meet the principal, and all I remember from that introductory meeting was his saying, "We don't expect you to teach them anything; just keep them from killing one another." But, did that daunt me? No, things couldn't really be that bad. Besides, I was different. I "understood" kids. My period of internship had been given an "A" by both my supervising teacher and the college personnel. They had hired the right person! After meeting the classes, I learned quickly that it was not unusual to call the roll and be informed that a missing student was "in for thirty." Not only did I have educationally challenged students, but many of them were involved in criminal activity! Enthusiastically, I would visit students in jail and take them books, which they couldn't read, and snacks. I sincerely wanted to become a good teacher.

The local newspaper sent a reporter to the school to interview and photograph members of the innovative Non-Graded Team program that teachers and administrators were traveling for many miles to observe. I felt honored that I was selected to be the model for the photography. I sat nonchalantly on my desk and gathered my students around for a hands-on activity which was mostly staged for the pictures. The article was printed, and I clipped it and sent it to my parents. I had succeeded! First year of teaching and their daughter had made the newspaper! It all looked good in print, but I knew that I was failing, and I didn't know how to change my methods.

I was given no in-service, no training, no peer mentor, and no support, not even a casual inquiry as to my progress or lack thereof. I had students who wrote in nonsense syllables, even for a spelling test, and I had no idea how to help them. I was reluctant to admit my misgivings to the other teachers on the team because they all seemed suave enough to have graduated from a finishing school. I was expected to write my own units for which I had no previous training. I felt like a lost ball in high weeds as my husband would say. I had no models from which to judge my performance or assess the performance of my students. As a result, I became extremely distraught and unhappy and submitted my resignation at the end of the year. I had failed to successfully cross that bridge from expectation to realization, so I quit!

I spent the summer feeling unfulfilled and considering myself a failure. Forgotten was my success as an intern because somehow that didn't count. When fall came, I missed the classroom. After all, I had been in school for as long as I could remember and fall meant returning to school. I applied for substitute teaching, and it was here that I learned how to be a teacher. In dealing with a different set of students every day in a classroom environment, I was able to observe the effects both negative and positive of teachers, some dedicated and some not so committed to the task. The results were tangible and readable in the classroom in the absence of the teacher.

All through our careers, we will have to clean the files to rid ourselves of accumulated garbage. The upswing of this activity is that we make room for the more positive aspects of our relationships and associations. After emptying the trash from our systems, it must be replaced with the nourishment meant for the mental and emotional well-being. If I had given up entirely on education after that one year, I would have missed much pleasure that I have experienced in the classroom. Substitute teaching allowed me to make an intermediate step to another level of thinking. Choosing the thoughts that we allow to play around in our heads is a major step in the direction of happiness. I understand that the school administration assessed the Non-Graded approach to teaching the "at risk" students and dropped it. Perhaps if I had been a little tougher, I could have overcome the hardships, disappointments, and feelings of failure in that first year.

A major danger in using fantasy as an escape mechanism is that of carrying fantasies into our personal lives and finding ourselves unhappy with the realities we face. I once associated with a young couple who seemed to constantly attract unhappiness on holidays. When asked, "How was your holiday?" the answer was usually filled with gloom and disappointment. The wife conversed with me on a particular Mother's Day and unknowingly revealed one of the causes of her stress. Sadly, she related that she had expected a certain new dress for which she had given ample hints, but she had received only flowers from her husband on her special day. Since she felt very special as a young mother, her feelings were hurt, and she felt unappreciated.

Immediately, I understood that she had set an expectation that may or may not be met by the uninformed husband. Some people, which could include husbands, seem to have great difficulty when it comes to perceiving and implementing "hints." She had fantasized the moment in which her loving husband would bestow on her the chosen gift or would lead her into that prearranged romantic evening to celebrate a special day. Rarely does the reality meet the expectation of the fantasy. Therefore, when her dreams did not come to reality, she was disappointed, and the husband was left feeling inadequate in his happiness-producing efforts.

In a gentle manner, I let her in on a little secret: Treasure the sentiment for the special day, but do not anticipate anyone's role except your own. If she did not anticipate the other's actions, she may enjoy the gift of his choosing. Actually, I told her to expect nothing and to be happy for any remembrance! Later, she thanked me and smilingly told me that she had adjusted her expectations, and holidays had become happier occasions. The error of basing our happiness on our expectation of what others may or may not do can be damaging to the happiness account. We may expect some sort of recognition for a special project and feel hurt if our accomplishments go unnoticed.

Likewise, a teacher may start out expecting to be rewarded and appreciated for work in the classroom. Of course, we all work hard and our audience is small. Our performances may be brilliant, but who is there to applaud? Feelings of being unappreciated can impede our creativity and allow for the mundane existence of every day becoming the same. These feelings may be accented through one phone call from a parent who is upset about a student's grade. One irate parent can crush our last shred of sanity. To suffer the judgment of someone less equipped than we are may strain our nervous system beyond endurance. In order to survive, the teacher has to rise above the written job expectation or description to see the greater picture. A teacher's self-respect and worth is not based on a single parent's opinion.

On the other hand, a teacher who is always expecting the administration to solve the problems, discipline the children, tailor the curriculum, and provide ideal working environments is living in a fantasy world. We may be fortunate to have most of the above, but the administration is not responsible for the happiness of the teachers. Blame shifting may give a temporary cleansing, but we all have to live with the circumstances that surround us. It is our choice as to whether we turn sour and smell or whether we are gracious and bask in our blessings.

Dealing with life as it is handed to us is not always easy. In the early nineties, I had a friend in the English department who had a daughter who was dying with leukemia. The young college student had earlier suffered with Hodgkin's disease and had been in remission. The mother felt close enough to me to share her frustrations and fears and grief at the time this 21-year-old daughter was diagnosed with leukemia. The mother would rush from the classroom to the hospital to spend a few precious hours with her dying daughter. On one particular day, the mother rushed into the hospital room and spent some time listing all the things that had gone wrong with her day. The daughter just lay on the bed and seemed to listen passively to the mother's account. Finally, the mother concluded her exhaustive list with the words, "I've had a bad day!" Then, she turned to her daughter and asked, "How has your day been?"

The daughter smiled serenely and said, "Mother, all my days are good. I have so few of them left that I can't afford to have a bad day." That mother grew a foot in character that day. She later told me that she made a vow to never again say that she is having or has had a bad day. It goes back to the adage of complaining of having no shoes until seeing a man with no feet. My friend consciously made a decision to have no more bad days.

Losing grip on our fantasies and dreams may come over a period of time instead of experiencing a sudden jolt as a new teacher. After a few years (maybe ten), a teacher may experience a period of "burnout." Teachers nearing retirement may be heard to say, "I just hope I can make it four (or another number) more years." All dreams seem to be buried, and they are just playing a waiting game. After 25 years of teaching psychology, one teacher retired, stayed out a year, and returned as the receptionist in the front office. When asked why she retired, her answer was always the same, "I just got tired of being responsible for students, for grades, and for discipline." I asked her if she ever regretted her choice, and she gave me a firm "no." Still, other teachers remain involved in innovative projects until their last day of service and may even go beyond the year that they could retire. If all fantasies have become grounded, the teacher must look for a new challenge in order to remain happy in the classroom.

Holding on to our fantasies, not to be confused with goals and objectives, may give us some measure of pleasure and relief, but fantasies do not produce growth or happiness. The teacher who remains tough and determined during the hard times without harboring resentment will learn from the lessons of life and will experience leaps in character development. Happiness depends on our overcoming the problems handed to us and working toward solutions. Somewhere in my memory are the words, "if life hands you a lemon, make lemonade."

Suggestions for Bridging the Gap Between Fantasy and Reality

1. St. Francis of Assisi wrote a prayer that is worth memorizing. "God grant me the serenity to accept the things I cannot change, the courage to change the things I can, and the wisdom to know the difference."

2. When an unpleasant task is given to you and there is no way that you can graciously decline, accept it without complaining and get to work.

3. Analyze your thoughts and take only those which are productive.

4. Find a special interest group that coincides with your preferences and explore the possibility of joining. A group may be labeled as "cliquish," but usually they are tight because of shared interest, not because of exclusiveness. A person once told me, "I make no friend among work associates as a rule!" This sounds good, but if we aren't friends with the people with whom we work, who are our friends going to be? Of course, we may get hurt from time to time, but "nothing risked is nothing gained."

5. If you have no lounge or gathering area in your school, look around for an unused nook and ask about designating it as a service area for teachers.

6. Ask your coworkers what they are doing in the classroom. Someone will be excited about a new project or presentation. Visit that classroom during your planning period and observe. Borrow some excitement to accent your presentations.

7. Refrain from carrying school problems into your personal life. None of your family members and none of your friends can do a thing to help you except be the object of your venting.

Building Classroom Relationships

A teacher's room is a second home. Care should be given to creating a pleasant environment for the teacher as well as the student. The classroom should reflect the tastes and interest of the teacher, not just the student. If the teacher makes the room belong exclusively to the children, they will overrun his or her space. One year I ran a little space experiment with seniors. I had a room with two closets, so I designated one large, walk-in closet for student use. I put supplies, some books, and things of interest in that closet. I told them that the closet belonged to them, and they could take what they needed without asking. One day, a student looked at me and grinned as he was walking toward the closet. "What's funny?" I asked. He answered, "I'm just going to visit my closet." A little part-ownership in the room was comfortable for both of us.

Space in the classroom is clearly defined. In kindergarten, students learn to respect the space of others, but there is a little space that belongs to each one. Ownership emerges much like that of owning one's name. In the high school classroom, squatters' rights are established early, and students feel protective of their space. When the teacher establishes boundaries and guidelines for the space that each student wants to maintain as personal, that space will be respected. One year I had a sophomore class that was unruly to the point of frustration. It seemed that they were everywhere and into everything. So, in order to maintain discipline, I shifted to the extreme and announced, "This is MY room; I live here all day long, and you just visit for a period of the day." I have to admit that my proclamation created a strained relationship. After a few days of commandeering the classroom, I relaxed the restrictions, and students began to settle into a more relaxed, yet structured, routine. No one method will work for all classes. Experimentation, even for seasoned teachers, is necessary.

In the late 1980s our district began to push the idea of cooperative learning within the classroom. In workshops, we were encouraged to implement group learning strategies. One morning, not realizing the students' attachment to their sacred space, I set the chairs in circles of five before the students arrived in order to implement a cooperative learning unit. As they entered the door, they looked (a) frustrated, (b) frightened, (c) disoriented, (d) unhappy, (e) betrayed, (f) all of the above. Of course, the answer is "all of the above." I had violated their space. Nobody was happy. No learning occurred that day much less cooperative learning. My feelings about cooperative learning were very negative until I learned that if I let students enter the room as usual and allow them to form the circles, it became their plan, their space. It was worth the extra time to arrange and rearrange the furniture each period.

After making the decision to be happy in the classroom, a big change came in my attitude toward my students and toward the actual time spent within the room. I began to decorate the walls with things that I like, posters that produce pleasant thoughts and memories. I brought some favorite books from home and made a sharing shelf for my students. I set up a lending system and allowed them to check out books from my collection. They were very faithful to return them. One of the students' favorite choices from the shelf was my high school yearbook. What fun they had comparing my senior class to their grandparents' pictures! The classroom became a cooperative experience, but it maintained my tastes and preferences.

Teacher happiness can be accented through the room environment, but conditions may negate the creating of the perfect classroom. For example, a floating teacher usually has no control over what is in the classroom or in its physical appearance. My second experience in public school teaching came 19 years after becoming a first-year-teacher dropout. I resigned my position in Corbin, Kentucky, in a highly academic private school, to move to Orlando, Florida, in 1989. The previous four years had been spent teaching honors classes, and my pride was the senior class of 19 students which proudly boasted seven National Merit finalists for the 1988-1989 school year.

On the other end of the academic spectrum, the teaching position that I was assigned in Orlando consisted of three classes of regular English II and a journalism class which incorporated the school newspaper. I wish I could tell you that I made the transition with great ease, smiling all the way. Not so! None of my previous teaching experience prepared me for regular English in a large high school in rooms with makeshift walls and no doors. And when I say rooms, I mean rooms. I floated into four different rooms within the math department. No peer teacher was assigned to me because I had come very "highly qualified"!

Behavior problems surfaced quickly. I would prepare a lesson, try to do a little lecturing, assign some reading, ask for discussion, but there was no positive response. At home, I expressed my frustration to my husband and sons. One evening the words tumbled out, "Today, I had a heart-to-heart talk to my worst class," and tears welled up in my eyes while relating the story. My son, age 14, said, "Mom, you're going about it all wrong! If you ever drop one tear in that classroom, you are dead! You will have lost it! It will become a challenge for the students! They will say, 'Let's see how long it will take to get her to cry today!'"

He was echoing the principal in my first teaching position who had told me that I needed to "toughen up," to which I replied, "That's not my nature." At the fresh, young age of 24, I didn't have the courage to deviate from my "nature" and become the teacher that those "at-risk" students needed. The principal even went on to say that I just may not be cut out to teach school. But this time, I had no intention of resigning, and I realized that whining was not going to make a pleasant working experience for me, my students, or my family.

I limped along for a few weeks, trying every motivational technique, every strategy, and every method adaptation in my scope of knowledge. My worst class, last period of the day, of course, was still bad in behavior and academic performance. To make matters worse, the principal's daughter was in that class and she was failing! Out of desperation, I stood before that group of uninterested, unmotivated, and inert students and said matter-of-factly and without tears, "I am a failure. I have tried to teach you great literature; I have tried to improve your vocabulary; I have tried to teach you to improve your writing skills so you can get a decent job; I have lain awake at night and worried about your grades, but I still have not succeeded. I don't know what else to do. So, I want each of you to write me a letter and tell me what I can do to improve my teaching methods."

I had their attention! I sat down at the desk and ignored them. They began to take out paper and start writing. The classroom was totally quiet. Jason, who was a senior retaking the class, stayed awake for once. Mike, who spent every period drawing on his art tablet, started writing! A miracle was unfolding before my eyes! The results were overwhelming. The writings were well-structured. Most of the students took responsibility for their behavior; some even included apologies. Many letters included compliments of my teaching, and several students took the blame for not applying themselves. Almost every letter included a suggestion on how to improve the class. Incredibly, this was by far the best writing that these students had performed all year.

I was ecstatic. By some miracle, I had the wisdom not just to accept the compliments and think all was well in sixth period English II. The next day I started the class by saying, "Thank you for your supportive letters, and I don't feel as though I deserve all the compliments that you gave to me, but I appreciate them anyway. But, most of all, I thank you for your suggestions on how I can improve the classroom activities. Today, we are going to follow one of John's suggestions which was to show more videos." Suddenly, they had a part in the planning. I don't remember the video, but that was not important that day.

That class had an amazing turn-around. Somehow, those letters communicated that we were a team. The barrier between the teacher's desk and the students' desks dissolved, and I found myself sitting beside students doing one-on-one coaching. Eventually, I was able to implement cooperative learning. Grades began to improve. Parents began to call with compliments on their children's progress. I've been given difficult teaching assignments since then, but I never forget that I am in charge and that the climate in the classroom is my responsibility.

Sometimes teachers are assigned almost impossible job tasks. They have the hardest-to-teach children, and it is tempting to make derogatory remarks concerning their abilities and actions. I've heard teachers and administrators refer to students as garbage, buzzards, idiots, and other unpleasant names. If we really think of students in these terms, it is going to be very difficult to establish a pleasant relationship in the classroom. To develop a compassionate attitude may be difficult because the teacher must experience the daily complications of working with the problem students. Someone once said, "Never tell children that they are not doing their best because they are doing their best. They are doing the best they can at the time." That statement is difficult to digest. We've been told to never criticize someone until we've walked a mile in his or her shoes. Maybe they are doing their best! As a teacher, we cannot see or understand all the garbage, baggage, and hardships the students bring to the educational process. They are affected by their past as well as their present circumstances.

In one English II textbook, the poetry is arranged thematically, and there is a section on death. One particular spring, I initiated the poetry unit with readings from the "death" poems. One selection actually described family members at the funeral of the father figure. During this reading, suddenly Todd jumped up and ran from the room. Immediately concerned, I sent a student to check on him. Another student explained that Todd's father had died of a heart attack during spring break and had actually breathed his last in Todd's arms! Imagine my chagrin! When Todd returned at the end of the period, I simply apologized and told him there would be a different lesson plan the next day. He was understanding of my position and was appreciative of my consideration for his loss. How could I say that Todd was not doing his best at any point in time? Intelligence quotients and achievements tests do not always reveal a person's operational potential.

One weekend, I was scheduled to attend a women's retreat just south of New Smyrna Beach. I decided to go a day early and spend the day writing. After arising early the next morning, I stopped at a Friendly's Restaurant on my way to the beach. Suddenly, the peace of the morning was shattered as 11 noisy high school-age students rushed past me and seated themselves in several empty booths. They were seated in two and threes, and one loner sat by himself. Close on their heels came the teacher who began barking orders in a sergeant-like manner. In record time, she had them all reseated into three booths. Looking slightly harassed, she informed the waitress, "I need coffee now!"

The students settled down, and she began to relax. She walked past my booth and seemed friendly enough, so I ventured, "Obviously, you are a teacher." "Yes," she explained. "These are 'at-risk' students," and she continued to tell me a little of her job description. On my way out, I stopped by her booth to chat a moment and explained that I was writing a book on teacher happiness. "What makes your day?" I asked. Immediately, she smiled and with a beaming expression toward her charges, she replied without hesitation, "My kids!" She continued, "When I see them accomplish a task, my day is made! If they would give me just an extra hour with my kids instead of all that paperwork, that would be the greatest gift." As I left, she was relaxed and enjoying the prospect of breakfast with her students. That morning, I met a heroine. She will probably not be featured in a magazine or even the New Smyrna local newspaper; nevertheless, she is a champion!

My schedule last year included one regular English II class. All sophomores in Florida have to take a state-required essay test in the spring called Florida Writes (now called FCAT Writing). In preparation, each English II class had to write a practice essay which was graded by an administrator. My class was below par in writing skills, so I coached them in writing techniques and drilled them in preparation for the test. They worked hard on the practice essays, and we eagerly awaited the results. Every day, someone would raise the question, "Mrs. Prewitt, do you have our essays back yet?" They couldn't understand what was taking the administration so long, and each day the anticipation mounted.

A few days later we received the graded essays along with a grid that charted how the students placed. By using a little calculation, it was simple to ascertain which set of scores belonged to my students. We had placed second (in a school of 4,200 students), not second for regulars, but second among all the sophomore classes, including honors. Smiling broadly, I announced to them that they had come in second on their essays that were graded by the administration! They smiled! They cheered! Their excitement was clearly visible. One large boy left his chair, came into the center of the room, got down on one knee and almost tearfully said, "Mrs. Prewitt, I have never been second at anything!" The whole room cheered as though he had just been presented a trophy.

These students were in such a state of excitement with their success that they would willingly write anything I asked of them. They could hardly wait to take the real test. Somehow in that practice test, we had become a team. Whether the motive was to impress the administration or to respond to a competitiveness within the sophomore class, these students rallied to the occasion.

Our classroom environment will be influenced by our perception of the students. Our attitudes often reflect the training we have had or the leftovers of someone else's experience. One year in May at a small college in Barbourville, Kentucky, where I was teaching, the Vice President for Academic Affairs was scheduled to speak at the end-of-the-year awards banquet. The next morning, one of my colleagues was lavish in his praise for the great speech made at the banquet, and he expressed regret that I had not been able to attend. Usually the banquet affairs were very stuffy and boring, so my interest was kindled in regard to any speech that was good enough to be the subject of discussion the next day. Curiously, I dropped by the speaker's office, told him of the accolades in circulation, and asked for a copy of the speech, which he gladly gave me.

The premise of his speech was that people can be divided into two categories: swamps and tractors. "We fall within either one or the other," he had said.

According to this educator, tractors are the doers who go out and conquer the obstacles and are rewarded with success. The swamps are those who are the passive members of society. They remain stagnant. I suppose he was referring to all those students who had received an award that evening as the tractors. He went on to tell the tractors that they should not waste their time on the swamps. If a tractor tries to plow in a swamp, the water will just return, and there will be no evidence that the plow had even been applied. His speech was suggestive that we leave those who cannot help themselves to chance, a type of "survival of the fittest" message. At the time, my husband and I operated an emergency shelter in our home for juvenile delinquents, the "swamps" of society. If we could make a difference in one child's future, we didn't consider our work in vain. If we could show a little compassion and guidance in a child's developmental process, we still felt that we were contributing to society. If everyone adopted this administrator's philosophy, what would become of our social system?

What kind of speech was that? Why did he receive such high acclaim among the professors? Granted, it was entertaining and well written, but what message did it send? Maybe the teachers felt "off the hook" for any failures in their grade books. After all, perhaps they had been plowing a swamp! Did this concept take away accountability?

Such an approach may bring an immediate relief to stress, but soon it is replaced with questions. What if there is a dry season in which the swamp will recede and the soil is tillable? History is full of successful people whose early life did not produce the slightest indicator of productivity. They could have been labeled as "swampland" and left to stagnate. These are the situations in which a teacher can be the factor that produces the metamorphosis. Teaching is more than the transference of knowledge. It is the ability to interact with the student to make that knowledge come alive and to find ways to implement that knowledge in a way that it becomes relevant and applicable to that student's life.

One year my schedule included a class of unmotivated sophomores. At the first of the term, I conducted one of those serious lectures and made the prediction that "this will be the year that your 'light bulb' will come on." I referred to that life-changing "light bulb" so many times that it became a joke among the students. Any idea that surfaced was labeled as the famous "light bulb." One day a "light bulb" came on for me. Why couldn't we create a poetry publication? The students met the challenge with great enthusiasm. Mike volunteered to draw the cover, Shemika wanted to choose the clip art, Sean wanted to write poems, some wanted to work in groups on poems, and Jon named the proposed booklet, "Dream Poems." The students organized themselves into a publishing company.

Finally, the poetry book was printed! I used it as a supplemental text since each poem had a recognizable poetic feature, if nothing more than imagery. The students were ecstatic in being published and having their work as part of the lesson plan. A few years later, a young man rushed up and hugged me in Publix supermarket. It was Mike, the artist. "Mrs. Prewitt," he exclaimed, "that light bulb you kept telling us about has finally come on for me. I'm at Valencia Community College now and am planning to become a youth pastor." His big grin filled my heart with the joy of accomplishment. Not long after that, my husband and I were seated at The Olive Garden, and the host looked intently into my face and asked, "Are you Mrs. Prewitt?" "Yes," I replied. He immediately turned to two co-workers and reported, "Treat this lady to the best in the house. She is the English teacher who taught me that I can write poetry." Sure enough, it was Sean from the "light-bulb" class.

I have done some research into the life of a particular Kentucky hillbilly. If you should read the following quotation without any clue that you may be reading an excerpt from an influential man's life, you would probably label him a "swamp" by the standards of the college vice president. Looking back on his life, this famous Kentuckian recalled the year that he began the seventh grade. "When I started to class that fall, they had algebra in our arithmetic. Well, I couldn't conceive any part of it. The only thing I got out of it was that 'x' equaled the unknown quantity. I thought, 'Oh, Lord, if we got to wrestle with this, I'll just leave—I don't care about the unknown quantity.' So my school days ended right there, and algebra's what drove me off" (from *Kentucky Living* June 1995).

How many educators would worry more than a few minutes over a slow student who dropped out? This boy was Harland Sanders who became the Colonel Sanders of Kentucky Fried Chicken fame. His father had died and he was having to help with the family care and support. Algebra seemed to be the back-breaking straw. Whether he found anyone else who believed in him, he believed in himself. He may have missed algebra, but he experimented for many years until he put together a formula that made him a millionaire.

During my research, I borrowed the video, *The Colonel Comes to Japan*. In the Japanese culture, employees are hired for life, which bolsters their morale and confidence. Workers will say, "I belong to KFC," rather than, "I work for KFC." In spite of the dedicated workers, the spotless kitchens, and the most desirable locations, Kentucky Fried Chicken was not selling in Japan. One of the promoters brought one of the life-size figures of Colonel Sanders and put it at the entrance of his restaurant. Immediately, that particular restaurant was in popular demand. More figures of Colonel Sanders were shipped and placed at restaurant doors, and business boomed.

One of my former college students furnished a humorous story in a narrative essay. He told of a particular night in his native Japanese city that he had too much to drink. He recalled bringing a friend home for the night and helping the friend stretch out on the couch before he went on to his bed. The next morning he awoke to find one of the life-sized images of Colonel Sanders lying on his couch.

The need to identify with a personality is the same in the classroom. The learning environment can be enhanced with the purchase of materials, furniture, and supplies. We can dress it up with posters and the greatest bulletin boards, but the most important factor in that scene is the teacher. Students need validation from that teacher. Teachers need validation from the students. Teaching and learning is affected by the relationship of the trainer and trainee.

One motivational speaker from the field of education told of a time in his early teaching experience when he was teaching very low achievers from poverty-level families in an all-black school. He extended an invitation to all the students to come to his house for dinner. When they arrived, they were ill at ease and a little overwhelmed with his "fine" home as seen through their eyes. When he took them into the dining area, they were surprised to find tables set up with white linen and the very best dinnerware that he possessed. Reluctantly and unsure they took their seats, and one boy picked up his fork and asked him, "Isn't this the dishes you would use when you have company?" The teacher answered, "Yes, I'm using my best dishes and silverware because you are the best company I could have." He went on to relate that the students' achievement level rose that year in unbelievable proportions.

One year I tried the teddy bear experiment. The idea came from a teaching video for beginning teachers. The instructions were to put a teddy bear in the room and make it accessible to the students for times that they needed a friend. I was toying with the idea when I visited our State Farm agent and saw a bear with a vest that read, "I'm your friend." Immediately, I decided to try the project and asked him if I could have one of his bears. Of course, he gave me one. In the beginning days of school, I introduced the bear by holding him lovingly and telling my tenth and eleventh graders, "This is Teddy; he is your friend. You can take him from the shelf and keep him at your desk on days that you need a friend."

You can imagine the looks, the chuckles, and one student even asked whether I thought I was teaching kindergarten. Nevertheless, I placed the bear on a shelf where he sat all alone for several days. Then, the time came when a student was very upset (boyfriend problem) and asked if could she have the bear. From that day, the bear was in constant use. One girl whose mother was dying with cancer asked me on a particularly stressful day if she could take the bear with her for the rest of the day. Soon, we had a bear shortage. The students began donating stuffed animals from their private collections. By the end of the year, we had a shelf full of stuffed animals, and they were in constant use by boys and girls. That was the warmest and fuzziest classroom of my teaching career. At the end of the year, I told them to take their animals back home or donate them. Those which were unwanted were claimed by other students until we had a clean shelf. It wasn't important that I know each student's problem, but it was comforting to them that they had a place to at least acknowledge that they needed a little helping hand.

Of course, we seldom have foreknowledge of our students' choices and achievements, but we must never forget that we are entrusted with the most precious asset that they possess. Even though they do not always present a suitable garden for the planting of the seeds of knowledge, we have to keep working. Every teacher could finish this chapter with a story of a student that required extra time, energy, and work. You could tell of the after-school sessions, the planning-period tutoring, the early-morning make-up sessions, and you would have your own success story to record.

To illustrate the message of this chapter, I will tell you about Tyrone. Tyrone first appeared on my rolls for English II. He was a basketball player who had just been bumped up to varsity, so his mind was on being a star, and the NBA was the goal. In the same class was his friend Andre who also had made the varsity team. Tyrone disliked English as passionately as he liked basketball. The major part of Tyrone's and Andre's classroom-passing strategies involved the solicitation of admiring females to either help them do their work or to actually do their work altogether. Andre had the advantage because his girlfriend was in the same class; however, Tyrone exuded such an aura of snobbery and independence that he found it difficult to be nice enough to get the favors. In fact, he didn't help himself in his relationship with me. He was disrespectful and expected me to pass him on his basketball ability. Tyrone and Andre were the top players and I love basketball. So, that year, my husband and I attended many of the basketball games, but Tyrone never acknowledged that I was there even though I knew that he was aware of my presence. On the other hand, Andre would mention that he saw me at the game.

Andre passed and Tyrone failed English II. The next year, I checked the rolls and there was Tyrone's name for English III. I assumed he had made up the English II credit in summer school. I volunteered for an after-school class designed for students who had failed English II and were falling short of graduation requirements and discovered Tyrone's name was on the roll sheet. Two hours a day with Tyrone was far from a thrilling thought!

But Tyrone came to class with an improved attitude. I thought, "Either he has matured over the summer, or he has learned that he can't slide through on his looks and skills in other areas." He worked hard that year and passed both English II and English III. I saw his friend Andre early in the year and casually remarked, "I have Tyrone again and he seems to be okay with being in my class a second year." Andre's reply gave me deep satisfaction, "Mrs. Prewitt, he told me that he was glad to be in your class again because he had felt badly about how he treated you last year, and he is glad for a chance to make it up." I was stunned! Tyrone did indeed make it up. Not only did he pass, but in the fall of the next year, I got a letter from the Outstanding Teachers of America organization, and the nominating student had been none other than Tyrone.

I am prouder of that letter that lists Tyrone's name as the nominator than I would have been in receiving any award they had to offer. This letter was proof that a bridge can be made to overcome whatever conflicts arise. I found Tyrone, then a senior, on campus and thanked him for the nomination. He simply said, "You deserve it, Mrs. Prewitt." I did something I was not supposed to do—I gave him a hug! Tyrone did not get offered the scholarship on the big campus that he coveted; however, he enrolled and played ball for a junior college, hoping to go to a four-college the next year. NBA is probably still a dream, but he has made some major strides in the right direction.

One tool in my classroom survival kit that has come in handy many times is my ability to never take anything personal that a child does or says. That concept can even apply to the unhappy parent who is accusing me of the student's failure. This is not a personal war; it would be happening to anyone in the same position of authority. It is amazing how objective I can become in a heated argument when I remind myself that this is not personal.

While teaching English III, I was contacted by an administrator with the news that a parent wanted a conference with me and an administrator, and the accusation that had been levied was that the child had told the parents that the teacher was a witch and was teaching witchcraft in the classroom. I had to laugh because I knew that I had taught *The Crucible* and *The Scarlet Letter* back to back, and each one deals with elements of witchcraft. Of course, as a literature teacher, I had taught passionately and had talked of superstition, ghosts, seances, and witches. Another interesting factor was that the daughter had made a low grade on the previous test.

Even though the father came with full intention, according to his own statement, of having me fired under the allegation of witchcraft, I did not accept it as a personal threat. I did not have to defend my existence as a witch or a nonwitch, for I was responsible for only that which affected the classroom. The administrator was helpful in explaining that every English III teacher would be teaching the same material. The father especially objected to a sentence in the introductory material that referred to a Puritan that might be a carpenter. He saw this as a reference to Jesus and was offended. Actually, another teacher had produced the handout and I had merely borrowed it.

After he finished with his accusations, I genuinely commended him for his interest and his desire to protect his daughter from harmful things. I reassured him that I was not teaching witchcraft. After a little time, he realized that he had been misinformed, and he felt ashamed and he apologized for his accusations. The daughter was a little embarrassed the next day, but I managed to smile as she came in and greet her in a friendly manner. It was never mentioned again. Because I did not treat the student's actions as a personal affront, we were able to have a good relationship for the rest of the year.

We may remember and use quotations from notable men that range from "Never give up!" to "Never say *never*!" If we apply that direction to the life of a child, we may see more "swamps" turn into tillable soil. The word *accountability* is sometimes resented in the sense that school administrators may use it to threaten teachers who are not performing in the classroom, but we are indeed accountable for those students who are dependent upon us to guide them through the educational process. If I give up on a child, the next teacher will have twice the task of preparing that student for learning. There is a lot of work to be done before the seed is ever planted.

An assistant superintendent of schools for North Carolina was asked to speak to all Orange County teachers at a giant rally in the University of Central Florida Arena. His manner was very relaxed, and he began to speak to that large audience as though he were just chatting with friends. Soon, I came to the realization that he was saying some things I wanted to write down, and I want to share this one thought. He said, "Children are not what you think they are; children are not what they think they are; children tend to become what they think you think they are." This statement puts a lot of responsibility and accountability on the teacher.

One morning as my husband was conducting business at the newspaper office in Corbin, Kentucky, an employee asked him if he were the husband of Mrs. Prewitt who taught at Union College. After his acknowledgment that he indeed was, she shared her story. "Your wife is the reason I'm working for the newspaper. I was a student in Mrs. Prewitt's freshman English class, and she told me that I should consider writing as a career. At the time, I had never thought of a career in writing, but if she thought I could write, maybe I could. She gave me the confidence to try, so here I am. I write a weekly column." Sure enough, I found her column in the paper along with her picture and her own byline. Certainly, I was proud of her accomplishment, but, at the same time, I felt a little apprehensive. Who was I to plan or recommend a student's future choices? Fortunately, she was happy with her choice and accomplishment.

We know that students are affected by association in the classroom, but I think that we diminish the extent of influence that we have. Many days those students spend more time with us than they do with their parents. The only smile or word of encouragement they may have that day is from us as we greet them or tell them goodbye. Likewise, as we develop that relationship with the students, they will contribute to our lives. We have all experienced times with those special students which often become wonderful memories.

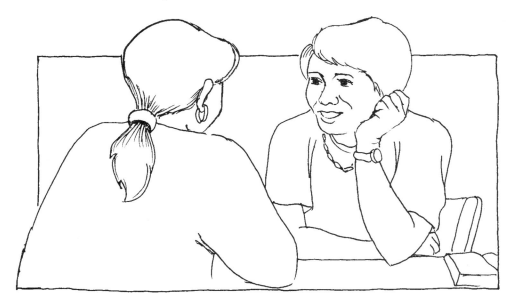

Suggestions for Building Classroom Relationships

1. Take the time to greet students individually as they enter the classroom and call a goodbye to them as they leave.

2. Learn their names quickly and use them as you greet them. Dale Carnegie writes, "A man's name is to him the most beautiful word in any language."

3. Make a point of greeting your students when you see them outside the classroom even if you are talking with another teacher. Take time to at least wave.

4. Give them time to share a little of their lives with you. Ask them about their weekend or vacation.

5. Try to avoid humiliating a student in private or in public. Humiliation may work to get regimented discipline because that child will have fear, but it will not work for a happy learning environment. Any person works better under praise rather than criticism.

6. Use language which will not be interpreted as judgmental. Allow students to share things that you find distasteful or against your own ethics. Giving guidelines is expected and mostly welcome, but a disapproving attitude will create a distance.

7. Resist the temptation to take things personally. One who takes things students or parents say or do personally may have difficulty with grudge-holding. Happiness tends to evaporate to make way for a grudge.

8. Always remember that each student has his or her own hardships and handicaps. It may help them to have a set time and place to talk about their problems.

CHAPTER 5

Making the Most of Restrictive Circumstances

We may take a journey and do research among people who geographically are what we consider trapped or cut off from the mainstream of life. We may find others who are confined or limited as a result of their circumstances or station in which they are born or have created for themselves. Still others are living in worlds too small whose restrictions are self-imposed because of mental barriers. Lumping these conditions into a bundle and labeling them promoters of unhappiness would be a mistake. Nevertheless, unhappiness can result from enduring these restricted worlds.

We have no choice in the geographical location in which we are reared. We progress on the rate and level that is prescribed for us and are usually content. While visiting with relatives in an even smaller town, my cousin, who was a little older than I, taught the younger children this song:

> Oh, the bear went over the mountain;
> the bear went over the mountain;
>
> The bear went over the mountain,
> to see what he could see.
>
> Oh, the other side of the mountain;
> the other side of the mountain;
>
> The other side of the mountain
> was all that he could see.

The image of that bear leaving his side of the mountain, climbing the mountain, and crossing over the top to see what was on the other side is a picture that I still carry with me. The song meant that the bear found the other side of the mountain to be the same world or type of existence as the one he left. I clearly understood at even a young age what the analogy meant, but the picture of the bear crossing that summit to the vistas of the other side of the mountain, the would-be pot of gold at the end of the rainbow, stamped a permanent impression on my mind.

A pitfall that may cause teachers to become unhappy could lie in their unintended restriction of themselves to one side of the mountain. Their classroom becomes the safety net. To leave it presents too many dangerous encounters. Those teachers may complain when called upon to attend faculty meetings, department meetings, or workshops. Curriculum advances or new approaches to teaching may be met with high-level resistance. Subsequently, those teachers restrict themselves because they do not take advantage of what a new idea has to offer.

Once upon a time, we had a parakeet named Tweety who lived happily in his environment. He liked his home in the cage, but he also enjoyed sitting on top of his house and taking occasional excursions through the other rooms. Upon his return flight, he would land on a curtain rod which was above the cage, and he would then descend to the door of his cage.

Without asking Tweety's permission, we moved. We put him in the same corner of the kitchen in the new house, but there was a hitch in Tweety's flight plan; there was no curtain rod above the cage. Its absence was like taking out the runway for an airplane. Tweety must have had poor vision because at the end of his flights in his new home, he would literally crash into the wall where the curtain rod should have been. Finally, he retreated to his cage and would not come out except to sit on the top. Other behaviors changed, and we knew that Tweety was mourning his past environment.

Trying to find a solution, we bought Tweety a companion—a beautiful white, female parakeet that we named Snowball. The union seemed aimed for disaster at the outset because each bird took a corner and remained in sullen silence. The frozen atmosphere in the cage continued for the rest of the day. A casual observer would think that we had caged two stuffed birds. During the night, I was occasionally awakened by noises coming from the kitchen, but I went back to sleep without investigating. The next morning when I went into the kitchen, the birds seemed to be friends. Upon closer investigation, it was obvious that their "friendship" was a result of the previous night's battle. The bottom of the cage was littered with feathers—all yellow! I looked at poor Tweety and quickly saw that he was missing every tail feather. Not one of those long, beautiful feathers remained.

The birds got along beautifully from that day as long as Snowball got her way. She got the favorite toy and any other cage item she wanted. Tweety learned to patiently wait until she would get her fill of food before he even dared to venture to the food tray. A few pecks on the head never failed to put him in his place. I saw the definition of "hen-pecked" in action!

I think they found happiness in their arrangement. At times they would snuggle close and make soft, loving sounds. One thing they had in common; neither bird enjoyed life outside the cage. Snowball refused to leave the cage even though the door remained open for days. Occasionally, Tweety's memory would return, and he would climb out the door and scale the side to sit on top of the cage, but Snowball would scold him to the point that he would soon return. Obviously, Tweety learned to live without his curtain rod and was able to be content in the confines of his small world. I constantly tried to get both birds to take advantage of opportunities of freedom, but the "outside" was too frightening.

Several years ago in a bookstore dedicated to motivational materials, I purchased a little magnet which advised me to "Bloom where you are planted," and I made it a permanent decoration for my refrigerator door. One of my sons thought I liked it so much, that he duplicated the saying by buying me a plaque with the same quotation and hung it in my living room, constantly reminding me that wherever I am, I have a responsibility to keep expanding my options. Postponement of happiness to another time, another job, another city will guarantee that happiness will be just out of reach in the present.

In the early 1980s, I taught Early Childhood Development through a grant program with Union College in Barbourville, Kentucky. My students were teachers from a tri-county area, and the job responsibilities required occasional visits to the classroom of each teacher in the program. One teacher stands out in my memory as one who "bloomed" in her remote area. Dorothy taught in a head-start center in Harlan County, Kentucky, Appalachian Mountain area. To get to her school from the town of Harlan, I followed a road that wound around the mountain. In the eight-mile journey, I crossed the same railroad track five times, giving the possibility of getting caught by the same train five times. Rather than feeling exhilarated by this drive through the mountains, I found it depressing. The poverty level was astounding and the little shacks, some of which stood on posts anchored in the riverbank alongside the road, gave me the greatest feeling of hopelessness.

In a delightful contrast, from the moment of my arrival at the little head-start center, all gloom evaporated. Upon arriving at Dorothy's door, I was greeted with smiling faces and ushered into the classroom in a manner reserved for royalty. The children had been prepped to show me their latest projects. One day, Dorothy met me with a big smile and informed me that she was so glad I had come on that day because they were serving poke salad greens and cornbread for "dinner" (lunch). Talk about local color . . . .

In case you don't know, poke greens are a weed-type plant that grows wild, especially where the ground has been freshly turned or on poor ground such as railroad beds or in areas where the ground has been stripped for the mining of coal. Actually, they are quite good if prepared properly. Properly means that they are cooked until tender, drained, and fried in bacon grease with eggs scrambled into the mixture.

Dorothy never ran out of glowing reports of exciting activities or events or creations of her students. Her portfolio for the program was the best. Her enthusiasm never lagged. When it came time to sit for the all-day panel testing and interviewing required to receive her Child Development Associate Certification, Dorothy was ready. She came to the assessment in her best clothing and filled the room with the excitement of the challenge. Of course, she passed in all areas. Afterward, she insisted that I go with her to the one-and-only steak house in the area (back in the town) and celebrate her victory. You would think that she had received a Ph.D. degree. After the meal, she placed a little box that contained a gorgeous old pen in my hand. She said that it was a family heirloom, but to me it is a treasured token of appreciation and pride that cannot be matched with things.

Restrictive circumstances are not necessarily a product of geography or resources. Recently, Sharon, a veteran teacher, stopped by to chat about our district's provision of a Personal Growth Plan that is an available option for teacher evaluation. She informed me that for the last few years she had been in a rut. "I've done the same thing every year and I'm tired of it," she lamented. A teacher like Dorothy might think it a little strange for someone to run aground in such a land-of-plenty as Orlando. The old saying, "You can take a horse to water, but you can't make him drink" is true, but someone added, "But you can put salt in the oats." Some glimmer of light had shined into that rut that Sharon found herself wallowing in because as she was leaving, she smiled broadly and said, "But I'm hoping that this year is going to be different. I'm looking for something that I can look back on and be proud of. I want to be able to say, 'this year I accomplished something.'" Sharon is on her way to that accomplishment. One, she realized her dilemma; two, she made a decision to make a change; and three, she is looking for a plan. Sharon is making good her promise by signing up for innovative workshops and actively pursuing avenues to new ideas.

Goal setting is a topic that likely would appear in any motivational book. The importance of goal setting has probably been established and presented by every company and institution in existence. To add to any present knowledge of goal setting would be an impossible task; therefore, goals will be considered in relation to happiness. How do goals add or take away from the happiness account? Career goals for a teacher are easily identifiable. Each state and school district has requirements that must be met. When beginning teachers talk of goals, they are usually referring to passing required teacher tests or acquiring another degree. The more experienced teacher may want to certify in another subject.

Setting goals too high may create some discouragement if those goals show no progress or realization. I heard a young man quote, "If I must have my expectations in the sky, I must provide the staircase." For years I have taught students with low academic profiles, but if I ask them what they want to be, I will get the most astounding answers. It is not unusual to have a student who is absent a lot and failing in several subjects to state that he or she wants to become a marine biologist (a favorite career choice) or a pediatrician or an attorney. Even students who are better prepared rarely have a clue as to how they get from here to there. A case management counselor for juvenile court shared the same phenomenon. Students in trouble for a criminal act, failing in school with no evidence of the employment of achievement skills, will list such prestigious career goals as pediatrician, lawyer, gynecologist, psychologist, etc. It's rather amazing that none of them add school teacher to that list! As I heard one professor say, they are "living life without a syllabus."

Goals should be both intermediate and long range. What happens if aspirants fulfill their goals and have made no future plans? Unhappiness may result. Some people may be able to live the dream, but I tend to think that the highly motivated people who have topped their goal lists would have a type of post-partum blues in the effort to just sit back and enjoy the scenery. What happens after the master's degree has been received and that cap and gown is now hanging in the closet as a witness to that achievement? How can a teacher transmit that energy into the classroom, an area where no certificate accompanies the success?

I have a friend, Phil, who has known all his life that teaching would be his career. He relates that he watched his own teachers, even in elementary school, and would consciously decide if he would handle a particular situation in the same way the teacher had. Continuously, he planned his career. For many years, Phil has been living the dream. He takes pride in his subject matter and is constantly looking for innovative ideas and new projects for his students. He is continuously buying things that are subject-related to exhibit in his classroom. Since he has many of the same students for all four years of Latin, he changes the displays fairly often. Phil schedules special days for students to interact with the subject matter through dress, food, role-play, etc. Pictures of his students displaying their achievements are framed and posted on walls and bulletin boards. Every student will be photographed at some point of class involvement and will find his or her individual picture peering from a tastefully displayed collage. It is no wonder that these students affectionately call him "Uncle Phil."

Of course, word of his accomplishments travels and this born-to-be-a-teacher friend has been offered various administrative positions, but he always maintains, "I am a teacher; I've always been a teacher; I'll always be a teacher. That is just what I do." How fortunate are the students who manage to have this teacher on their schedule!

A science teacher, Matt, in my school relates that he changes all his lesson plans every year. "Why?" I asked. "Because I don't want to get bored! If I do the same thing this year that I did last year, I get bored and the kids are bored!" he replied. This teacher managed to get an old school bus for the purpose of shuttling his students back and forth to swamps, parks, woods, and other places. He literally has a traveling classroom. Matt told me that he and Henry David Thoreau would make a great team as curriculum writers. He constantly asks for resources from other members of the faculty.

In contrast, I once met a teacher who was desperately trying to escape the classroom and contact with students. He put in for a promotion to the administrative level. While waiting for this promotion, he made derogatory remarks about the students and even gave them labels such as trash and garbage. The promotion did not come, and he has become embittered and ineffective as a teacher. There was a goal, but no plan was made to master the intermediate steps of researching and adapting to the qualities that make a good administrator.

In addition to falling into a trap of setting goals too high and failure to make intermediate goals, we may set for ourselves a very low goal. We may take refuge in the little statement that "if we aim at nothing, we will succeed." That type of success would be very unfulfilling and would create unhappiness. Low goals are set at points when we are feeling low self-esteem. We feel inadequate; therefore, we expect very little from ourselves. A teacher with no goals or very low goals may tend to become a loner and withdraw from outside stimulation. Low goals should serve only as the beginning point, the basis from which to launch our future goals.

At the beginning of every school year, an initial assignment for my high school students requires them to write their goals for the year in relation to academics, extra curricular activities, career plans, and other areas of their own choosing. They select unrealistic goals at times, but there are those who honestly state that their goal is to "pass this class." For some, that may be a high goal while others would consider that a low goal. The assignment also asks for some long-term goals. Some will write a career choice such as lawyer or doctor. I encourage them to fill in the steps that will get them from here to there. Most of the time, they have very little knowledge as to the amount of education, the time involved, or the money required to realize the goal. However, the activity encourages them to think in terms of planning their goals at an early age. Students have a feeling of pride when they make the grade that they have projected on their sheet. They will often remind me of their successes. Furthermore, former students will meet me in the hall and give updates of their progress. A smile of happiness and pride usually accompanies the report.

We can start with a very tiny goal, just one goal and not several tiny goals. After reaching that goal, we are ready to move up the chart. There is no lifestyle so insignificant that goal setting cannot help the participant to enjoy life to a greater extent. The goal may be to read a recommended book. A goal accomplished, no matter how small, will bring a glow of happiness.

Lessons can be learned from everyday experiences. I learned one from a little packet of seeds. Between the ages of eight and twelve, my son, David, loved to plant flowers and watch them grow. He was the champion sunflower grower for miles around. After much fervent pleading, he persuaded his father to build a huge flower bed across the front of our house. In the springtime, he would cultivate it and plant new flowers. One spring, David was a little slow about getting the flowers planted. A lady in our church had given me what I thought was a package of mixed flower seeds to give to David. The flower bed was ready, but David had made very little effort at the planting stage. So, seeing the waiting, freshly turned soil, I impulsively opened the package and scattered the seeds in the soil. A little later David planted his flowers. Shortly thereafter, David began to complain about these odd plants coming up in his flower bed, but he let them grow. Eventually, he had a few radishes, a few carrots, a bean vine, and a cucumber vine that mysteriously appeared in his flowers.

Guiltily, I confessed my impulsive act and received the well-deserved scolding. "Mom, how could you have put something into my garden?" There are several lessons to teach and be learned here about messing in other people's gardens or acting impulsively, but I will overrule the temptation and stick to the subject. I humbly went out into the yard and cleaned the flower garden.

The lesson I want to share relates to the "bloom where you are planted" advice. The little innocent vegetable seeds had no idea that they were misplaced by being planted in the wrong garden. When they grew in their normal fashion, they did not look around and say, "I don't look like the others in this garden. Something must be wrong with me." No! They contentedly grew, totally ignoring all the obvious reasons why they should not grow successfully. Sometimes we may feel that we got planted in the wrong garden. One teacher-friend refers to hardships or difficult situations as going through a "desert" or a "wilderness experience." We can make all kinds of excuses, but I will try to remember the little vegetable seeds which were mercilessly planted in a flower garden. Their happiness did not diminish in the least because some thoughtless mother got impatient and made a boo-boo.

The students are the plants in our garden. They did not ask to be planted in our classroom; in fact, they had no choice in the matter whatsoever. The only nurture they will have is what we give them day by day. They are all different in their growth, their appearance, their purpose, and in the final product. It is our job to care for them, to apply fertilizer, to dig, and to prune a little. Just as that gardener shows pride in every stage of the growth process, we as teachers can take pride in our part of the achievements of our students. Their achievements are our credentials.

Suggestions for Broadening Our Horizons

1. Set some long-range goals for yourself.

2. Create a chart of intermediate goals to implement along the way. Make some goals low enough for easy and early achievements.

3. Browse through professional magazines in your library or media center. Do some reading to foster new ideas.

4. Interact with colleagues who are excitedly telling of classroom activities. You may not want to duplicate, but an idea may issue from the discussion.

5. Ask colleagues to permit you to sit in on a class.

6. Discuss your idea or ideas with someone, anyone. The activity of verbalizing will generate enthusiasm and help you put substance into the idea.

7. Integrate something new to YOU in your plans this week.

Improving Teacher/ Administrator Relationships

Students are always excited on the days that report cards are distributed. Even if students have been told the grades ahead of time, they still want to see them on paper. Some jump for joy over an unexpected A or B. Others may cry in pain over an unexpected D or F. Then the comparisons begin! "What did you get in art?" etc. Inevitably, teachers are challenged and must always be ready to give reasons and documentation for the particular grade that was recorded.

In the same manner, the teachers in Florida anxiously awaited the schools' first report cards, which were issued by the State of Florida in the summer of 1999. Not only did the schools receive the report, but the grades were distributed and published in the local papers for all to see. "A" schools were rewarded with big sums of money, and "F" schools were penalized by withholding program funding. Teachers in the "F" schools found themselves feeling degraded, and morale dipped dangerously.

Ultimately, school administrators feel the need to implement new programs of curriculum, assessment, and staff development with the objective of raising the grades for next year. As a result, the teachers may get caught in a sweep of activities to upgrade classroom performance. In many cases, the passion of the administrator is lost on the teacher who may be satisfied with his or her existing teaching methodology. Teachers may tend to vent negative response on a particular administrator and fail to realize that the administrator is simply following the blueprint that was given at a county or district or even state-level meeting. To criticize the immediate supervisor in regard to the new requirements or new documentation is similar to blaming a waitress for the chef's overcooked steak.

Motivational workshops are often overlooked in the scheduling of staff development for educators; however, teachers are begging for help in that area. In a recent meeting of resource persons, the leadership posed the question, "What do you need us to get for you?" A teacher from an "F" school stood up and said, "We need some motivational help! Do you know what it feels like to be labeled an 'F' school?" A situation of this type calls for teamwork between administrators and faculty to lay the groundwork for improvement rather than fault-finding and blame-laying.

For all of middle school and high school, my younger son marched with the high school band as a drummer. The drum line consisted of a tight group who saw themselves as an entity in themselves. When I would refer to him as a member of the band, he would say, "I'm not in the band; I'm on the drum line." Granted, the drum line made up a significant number of that three-hundred-plus-member band, but they were not a separate entity. The superior and detached attitude was evident in the group's behavior, and they were always in conflict with the band director and the overall program. On road trips, there was even the designated "drum-line" bus. To not be part of the band, it was rather strange that he participated with them at every football game, every competition, and every fund-raising event. His transcript shows four credits in band, not four credits in drum line. Likewise, teachers who have their own little groupings and begin to feel autonomous most likely will create problems for themselves and for the leadership.

Any successful organization or institution operates as a team effort. Every corporation has a flow chart, and each member of the team or staff has a slot on that chart. A sports team has to be divided into specialties and abilities, and a team that does not follow the coach will have difficulty winning. The football players who do not follow the signals issued by the quarterback will be reprimanded and may lose playing time. Whatever the group, there must be leadership. How well that team performs to a great extent is dependent on the members' acceptance of the leadership. Since teachers have their own classrooms and small groups of students, they are sub-leaders under the big umbrella of leadership. Teachers can become "king or queen of the castle" in their own room. However, if any teacher is walking out of step with the school's philosophy and mission, there will be conflict. Now that I have clearly stated my stand in regard to supporting my administration, I want to discuss some of the attitudes that can cause unhappiness for the teacher.

One difficult area for a teacher to accept is that of an administrator's not being as impassioned about a student's infraction as the teacher. The teacher experiences the emotions involved in observing or experiencing the offense; whereas, the dean or designated assistant principal merely reads words from a page. Early in my teaching career, I stumbled onto two students out of class without a pass (bad enough), and they were engaged in some heavy kissing. Seeing an administrator a little farther down the hall, I requested that the students accompany me. I explained the situation to the administrator, and then I made the mistake of waiting for his reply. Rather than addressing the students, he said to me, "They probably have come in late and are on their way to class." Of course, the students nodded in agreement, and we were dismissed.

I was steamed! I felt foolish! I felt discredited! My cheeks flamed, and I slinked back to my room to stew in my lair. "Well, that's the last time I will report any incident," I vowed. "What happened to the workshop training that strongly suggested that we are to teach values?" My mistake was in a lack of understanding for chain of command. If I were to be given the responsibility of judge and jury, then there would be no need of the assistant principal or dean.

When I comprehended that once I turned in the paper work and had relinquished the problem to a person in a higher position on the administrative chart and understood that the incident or situation ceased to be my problem, I had no trouble living with the consequences. An example from our judicial system may help us understand. When a police officer makes an arrest, his job is finished except for filing the report. He may be called into court for a testimony, but he has no jurisdiction or power over the outcome of the arrest. He does not serve as a juror or the judge. If that officer is unhappy with the outcome of the case, he suffers alone. He can accept that position, or he can grumble and complain and create unhappiness for himself and his associates.

A teacher shared with me her frustration in a similar situation. As a personal fitness teacher, she brought her class into a locker room that had been used by other teachers earlier in the day. One of her students came to her with a small tin that contained marijuana. Fulfilling her duty, she reported the find and turned in the evidence. Not only had she reported finding some marijuana in a locker room, she was sent by the dean to the other teachers to try to trace the owner. The other teachers, perhaps feeling defensive, offered no help and seemed disinclined to comment. She felt helpless because she had done her part, but no one else appeared to be concerned. Feeling frustrated and unhappy, she questioned whether she should bother next time to report such an incident. She could have escaped the frustration by leaving the evidence with the dean and "washing her hands" of the incident.

As teachers, our responsibility ends when the referral or report is made. We have relinquished the problem or case to a higher authority, one whose place on that organizational chart designates that an administrator's job is to determine the punishment to fit the crime. To agonize over the outcome will just make us unhappy and resentful. We may carry that resentment into the classroom, and the students will immediately perceive that we are at odds with the administration. An unexpected consequence could be a break-down of our authority as disciplinarian. I've read and heard

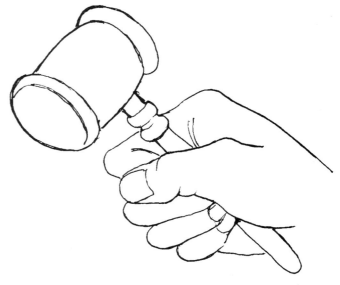

that a good leader must first be a good follower. After such an incident, the teacher may adopt a "see no evil, hear no evil, speak no evil" attitude. Not only does this approach break down the team effort, it contributes to the risk factor on a school campus.

Once a teacher is sure of administrative support, a conflict with a student or parent becomes easier to handle. The first time I was scheduled for a parent conference, the meeting was composed of a mother, myself, and the principal. The school where I was teaching is legendary as a highly academic private institution, and the mother was protesting her daughter's grade of B. I felt no support from the principal. She remained totally silent while I attempted to defend my testing and grading methods. The mother totally ripped me apart, accusing me of unfairness and partiality to other students, one in particular. I stood firm until she threatened to withdraw her two children. Having no previous experience of this type, I didn't know how to handle such a threat which now involved the finances of the school. The principal still offered no words of guidance for either party.

Finally, out of desperation, I said, "Okay, if you think your daughter should have an A, then she shall have it. You have graded her work, not me." Even though she was not quite satisfied, she had won her case. The principal never did let me know if I had done the right thing. As a result, I had constant fear of being challenged by parents. Fortunately, I believe that the incident resulted in my becoming a better teacher. From that conference, the realization and acceptance of my accountability for classroom activity and assessment caused me to make absolutely sure that I could document every learning activity, requirement, and assessment method and procedure. Most likely that principal was far wiser than I gave her credit at the time.

On the other hand, when an administrator can be counted on for supporting the teacher (as in the witchcraft story in chapter four) in times of confrontation, the teacher will experience a sense of strength rather than relying on defensive measures. It is much easier to admit our weaknesses and mistakes to someone who is supportive and helpful. Of course, if the teacher is wrong and will not take counsel, the administrator has a job to perform which may not be pleasant. The teacher's vision may be confined to the limits of the classroom whereas the administrator must nourish and protect the whole environment.

One fall, a retired military man was hired as a math teacher and assigned to the room next to me. The first grading period he showed me his grade sheets, and approximately eighty percent of his students had Fs. Immediately, I showed alarm because I knew, administratively speaking, that he was in a sinking ship. I tried to reason with him and inform him that his job would be on the line unless he showed a definite improvement for the next grading period. His answer gave me little hope. "They are expected to know certain things when they enter ninth grade math. If they do not and cannot keep up, I will not compromise the course objectives." No matter how many case scenarios I presented, he remained adamant in his resolve to reward their shortcomings with Fs.

Second grading period came, and his grade sheets reflected no improvement. As a new teacher, he didn't realize that in reality the grades were a reflection of his teaching. Of course, you know what happened! Students levied accusations, citing his "lack of proper teaching" and "inadequate explanations." Irate parents began to call. Of necessity, the administrators got involved. He reported all these activities with a seemingly amused attitude. I warned him that he would lose his job if he did not conform to the grading procedures and listen to the complaints and make some adjustments. He did provide after-school tutoring sessions, but if students failed to attend for whatever reason, he felt validated in his grading methods. He declared, "I refuse to compromise!" The rest of the story is evident. It came as no surprise to me that he received the notice of employment termination at the end of the year. Now he is bitter and abusively critical of school regulations, administrators, and the whole educational system, and since he is unemployed, he doesn't lack for time to brood on all the educational wrongdoings.

In order to be happy as a teacher, there is a certain amount of flexibility that is necessary for fitting into the workings of a school system. Acceptance of each person in his or her role is vital. A social studies teacher was heard voicing his complaints of administrators. "Why do administrators leave the classroom if they are so 'good'?" he asked. Immediately, he answered his own question. "Either they are not good at teaching, or they don't like kids, or they just get tired of teaching." With such a concept of administrative personnel, this teacher will never be happy with school leadership because he does not respect the position. A person who cannot accept authority and leadership will be unhappy with any person who accepts the title. The conflict is not personal. Again, happiness is a decision. We take the "bad apples" with the good, but we can't allow the bad ones to spoil our relationship with the good ones. That administrator who failed to support me (or so I thought) in that first confrontational parent meeting, later became a tower of strength in molding me into a better teacher. She forced me to grow. Thankfully, I didn't allow that first disappointment to color my perception of her role.

It is difficult to separate the person from the position. I was privileged to observe a classic case of respect for title in the House of Parliament in London, England. While observing from the visitor gallery, I noticed the members of Parliament stopping to give a short bow to an empty chair that graces one wall of the chamber. When a member would enter or leave, he would make a short pause of respect to an empty chair. Upon returning to the anteroom, I asked one of the guards or attendants why they bowed to an empty chair. "Oh," he answered, "they are not bowing to the Queen, but rather to the throne itself in recognition of the Royal House." So, whether they like or dislike Queen Elizabeth II is irrelevant to the act of allegiance which is given to the throne itself. Likewise, we as teachers do not have to agree with all actions of our administrators; nevertheless, they are our leaders and deserve a show of respect for the office they fulfill. (No, we do not have to bow!)

Another factor that can create poor team relationships involves our choice of associates. If we find ourselves in a critical group, it will influence the way we look at our leaders. Faculties are sometimes broken into little cliques. A new or transfer teacher may innocently fall into such a group. One faculty at a school where I worked was terribly divided. Unknowingly, at the first faculty meeting, I sat with the most disgruntled group. While the administrators were facilitating the meeting, there was a constant undercurrent of cutting remarks circling the group. Most of the derogatory statements came from the mouth of one person, but the others seemed to be in agreement. The insulting attacks were on the shortcomings of the administration. Feeling very uncomfortable, I decided that the next meeting would find me sitting in a different area of the room.

Car-pooling can also present opportunity for negative communication. I once had two riders who traveled with me over 20 miles each way to school. Both were unhappy with the administration. Being a newly hired teacher, I wanted to get into the flow of activities, so I bought a shirt with the school logo. On school spirit day, I wore my new shirt. Both teachers vented their hostilities all the way to work—20 long miles. I arrived on campus feeling depressed and defensive. This was my new home. I planned to spend many hours at this location. I wanted to be happy in my new job. Something must be done! That afternoon as we began the journey across town, I spoke my heart. "I'm glad to have you ride with me," I began, "but if you insist in saying bad things about the school and the administration, I cannot continue to bring you in my car." I went on to explain that I had no problems with them or with the administration.

It was quiet for a long time, but I held my ground. We had a lot of quiet drives, but there was no more airing of grievances in my car. Later in the year one of the assistant principals said to me, "Arlene, you are riding with two of the most negative people that I have ever known. How do you stand it?" I stood it because I had enough courage to draw the line.

It is possible that our level of self-esteem will determine how well we handle a situation. All people in leadership positions will have times when someone will challenge their authority or try to attack them as the leader. The measure of the leader's strength will be in the response to the attack. The key is not in reading books to help increase self-esteem or attending workshops. The answer to this attack is in how that administrator reacts. I once heard a church leader make the statement that no one could insult him. Wanting to hear more, I listened very carefully to his next statements. He continued, "You cannot insult me unless I allow it. Just because you say something derogatory about me doesn't mean I have to take it. Your power ends where my will begins." In one of the resource rooms of our media center, a poster hangs with the following quotation, "No one can make you feel inferior without your consent."—Eleanor Roosevelt

Many nights I have lain awake and fretted over a student's behavior toward me or a parent's accusation that it was my fault that the student was doing poorly. I asked my husband, who is in a leadership position, how he could seem so unaffected after someone had criticized or attacked him in an unfair way. His answer has served me well: "They are not attacking you personally; they are attacking the position. Whoever fills that role will have to contend with the problems. If you quit tomorrow, those accusers would lose interest in you immediately, so it is not you personally that is the object of their criticism."

Anyone who is happy in a leadership position whether teacher or administrator has learned never to take things personally. Many attacks are made at the position, not the occupant of that position. Teachers sometimes complain that a certain assistant principal passed them in the hall and didn't speak. That principal may be returning from a particularly distressing parent conference or student confrontation. Or it just could be that the principal may be on his or her way to a classroom that has an emergency situation in progress. It is generally a little embarrassing when we learn that we have hastily accused or criticized without knowledge of the circumstances and later learn the situation merited the offending action.

A teacher once said, "Everyone feels they have a right to complain or give opinions about education because that is something that we all have experienced to some degree." Parents constantly compare their days in school to their children's situations. Teachers may feel that neither the parent nor the administration can empathize with their position in the classroom. Administrators sometimes forget the drudgery and stress involved with a daily class presentation. The administrative team can sit in an exclusive retreat center during the summer and map out strategically great plans for the teachers to implement. In the fall, the returning teachers are not so enthusiastic about a new responsibility added to their already heavy load, and complaining can be a natural result.

If a problem remains unresolved, it is best to schedule a conference with the administrator and talk it out. Teachers may have difficulty scheduling with the administrator, who has not been furnished a secretary. They may get the feeling that they are being slighted and must catch administrators on the run because so much of their day is filled with duties and immediate situations. But most principals and assistant principals are at the school long after the last teacher has left. However, if teachers make it known that they need an appointment, I have never seen it fail that an audience is provided. The teacher may be inconvenienced a little with an after-school appointment rather than one scheduled during the planning period, but the interaction will be worth the inconvenience.

With computer technology in the classroom, the chance of misunderstanding may increase. E-mail messages are usually short and to the point, and they may convey to the reader a different tone from what was intended by the writer. If there is a problem generated by such a misunderstanding, a stroll down to that administrator's office or teacher's room for a little reassuring chat can ease tension and promote productive relationships.

Administrators are looking for team players. Finding teachers who will teach lesson plans is not the difficult chore. The teacher who wishes to remain isolated may develop resentment if asked to assist in some duty that is outside the classroom door. Some teachers feel resistance to attending a training session and take pride in "marching to the beat of a different drummer." On the other hand, an attitude assessment may illuminate a negative thought process, and we can start measures of correcting the behavior that is prohibiting our happiness. Once I aired a criticism of another teacher to a friend who immediately followed-up with a compliment for the teacher. I felt immediate shame for my words and resolved to put a bridle on my tongue. I've learned that I receive more joy from complimenting a colleague than in finding faults.

It is very difficult on all concerned to be part of a team and not be a team player. I'm reminded of a joke about a couple riding a bicycle built for two. After reaching the top of a long hill, the man turned around to his wife and said, "Whew! I thought we were never going to make it up that hill. There were a few times I thought we were going to roll backwards." The wife replied, "And we would have, too, if I hadn't put on the brakes." Finding your niche in a large environment may not be easy, but there is a place where your talents are needed.

Suggestions for Improving Teacher/ Administrator Relationships

1. Remind yourself where your duties end and the administrator's responsibility begins.

2. Once an infraction has been reported, support the administrative decision.

3. In group gatherings, associate with people who are enthusiastic and excited about the school.

4. Try to be a learner. Take advice and be flexible enough to change when necessary.

5. Offer your assistance to special projects or special days.

6. Request a conference to settle a difference rather than spread your unhappiness. Be respectful of time constraints.

7. Make your expectations of your administrators within the human realm. Understand that they also make mistakes and deserve a second chance.

8. Be slow to criticize. In *How to Win Friends and Influence People*, Dale Carnegie wrote, "Don't criticize anyone . . . . Any fool can criticize, condemn, and complain, and most fools do. But it takes character and self-control to be understanding and forgiving."

CHAPTER 7

Charting Discipline

In a recent meeting with curriculum resource teachers, the moderator asked the group to give suggestions for future workshops. "What are your needs?" she asked. One lady vehemently spoke her request, "Unless we get some discipline in our school [a ninth grade center], we are going to go under." Nobody commented on her outburst, and other teachers began to voice various needs as the moderator made a list. I suggested that we need some motivational input to improve teacher happiness. Immediately, the lady with the discipline problems spoke, "There will be no happiness until we get discipline in the classrooms!" Her deduction would most likely get a unanimous vote of agreement.

One beginning teacher became very stressed at the start of the year because his fourth period class was incorrigible. He asked the dean to visit his class. The dean who is known as an effective disciplinarian gave a speech to the class, and they all listened attentively. Feeling all was well, the dean left and chaos returned. I'm reminded of the cartoon character, Garfield the cat, who enjoys a friendship with the mice as long as his master isn't present. The next step the teacher made was to ask his advising assistant principal to visit the classroom during his "worst" period. The behavior was less than desirable and the teacher was frustrated.

On another occasion, I had the opportunity to observe this same teacher. It soon became evident that his greatest problem was that he never commanded the attention of the whole class at any one time. Some students were on task while others had no clue as to the assignment or objectives (if any). He didn't take attendance, so students drifted in and out at will, seemingly without his noticing. Like the teacher from the ninth-grade center, this teacher cannot be truly happy until he solves the problem of classroom management. Unfortunately, he wasn't happy and resigned the position after three and one-half months.

Even though it is directed to new teachers, Harry Wong's video set, *The Effective Teacher,* is an excellent resource for any teacher having difficulty with class management. If the videos are not available or not in the budget, the accompanying book, *The First Days of School,* can be purchased, and I highly recommend the expenditure. In his video, Harry Wong teaches that there must be some procedure in place for getting students' attention, and his own method is to just raise his hand and stand silently waiting for all students to respond. Of course, his video audience was all teachers that had been given the procedure, so when he raised his hand at the beginning of the session, they all responded and fell silent. He praised them, and I thought, "This isn't a valid experience. These are teachers!" Ironically, I have noticed in workshops that at times teachers are more difficult to bring to order than students.

In Florida it may stay hot well into October before we get any relief from the heat with what I call a "cool spell." A beginning teacher came to me at the beginning of third period and said, "My air conditioner isn't working and my room is very hot. Could my students possibly use your room for the rest of the day?" I walked down to his room, and sure enough, the thermometer was registering above 90 degrees, and the students were sweltering. It was obvious that no learning was going to take place that day.

We checked the breaker box and the thermostat settings, but nothing helped. Finally, I invited him to use my room. Since my room is utilized for staff development, there are many things accessible that the students would not find in an ordinary room. Before ushering them into my room, I wanted to give a little procedure announcement. So, with these very noisy and complaining students, I decided to employ a little Harry Wong instruction without their even being aware of the procedure. I asked the teacher if I may speak to his class. He nodded his consent, so I stepped in front of 30 very distracted and very unhappy eleventh graders. I just calmly raised my hand and made eye contact with those who looked toward me. Miraculously, the students began to quiet and in a matter of seconds, the room became totally quiet. Where was Harry Wong when I was a beginning teacher or even a ten-year teacher?

When I returned to high school teaching, I had grown accustomed to teaching in college where the teacher does not have to be concerned with discipline. It was soon apparent that I did not have a handle on classroom management, especially in regard to the first part of the period. How was I to monitor the hallway until the tardy bell rang, then take roll, answer questions in regard to make-up work, and get the class started on some type of instructional activity without having a lot of students disengaged from anything productive? Those first chaotic ten minutes of "housekeeping" activities were affecting the whole period. My son was in high school at the time, so I asked him about his English teacher. He seemed to think that she had no problems in getting the students on task.

My son's English teacher taught down the hall, so I managed to be unobtrusively stationed in the hallway near her door at the beginning of my planning period. There she stood, faithfully doing her hall monitor duties, but she was distributing copies of a handout as students were entering the room. She greeted each one as she handed them a piece of paper. Since the door was open, I could see the response. The students went to their seats and started reading the papers! Then they started preparing to do some type of work in response.

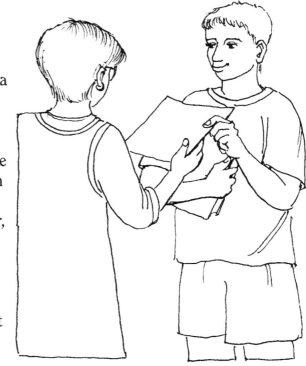

After school, when my son got into the car, I asked what his English teacher had given him as he went in the door. He said, "Oh, that was a question that she gave and asked us to write our response in a paragraph." Immediately, I thought of the grading load. "Does she grade these responses?" I asked. "No," he replied, "we put them in our notebook, and she takes them up ever so often and gives us credit." In later observations of this incredible English teacher, I noticed that she often rented costumes that represented the particular period of literature that she was teaching. One memorable morning, she graced her classroom with a gorgeous Elizabethan dress and wig. No doubt she had the students' attention that day!

I talked to another teacher who seemed to have it all together. In response, she shared her method of obtaining immediate class control. At the beginning of the year, she had introduced the procedure for getting the class immediately on task. Every day, she would write a statement on the board before students arrived. Each student kept a spiral notebook for journal entries, and they were responsible to write a response to her quotation or saying of the day as the first order of business. Occasionally, she would take them up for checking. This method automatically includes an absence penalty. If a student gets points for each day's entry and has several entries missing, there will be a penalty.

Lacking the organization to get handouts ready on a daily basis, I opted to try the journal approach. Amazingly, the students accepted this idea and worked on their journal response while I did the "housekeeping chores." If for some reason, I neglected to have a topic on the board, students would inevitably ask for the journal topic for the day. I realized that this time of sharing their thoughts was becoming an activity that was more than just a time filler.

Another little area of frustration for me was in the students' question of "what are we going to do today?" I would get funny and say things like "sing and dance," "order pizza," "have a party," and other goofy replies that left the students unamused and unanswered. One day, I decided to write the day's agenda on the board. If a student asked, "What are we doing today?" I merely said, "Read the board." Immediately that student became engaged in the day's activities. There is one drawback to this method. Advanced students can begin work and be far into the assignment before that unmotivated student even gets the message of what is to be done. However, that advanced student usually has learned how to make adjustments for the slower classmates. Sometimes, they work well as tutors or group leaders in cooperative learning.

Even though students may have to wait for the handout or whatever is needed to get the assignment activated, they want to know the agenda. When I internalized this new insight, I agreed that I feel the same way. I want to know what is on the agenda of a meeting. I even want to know what is on the menu for dinner. In more recent years, I developed interest areas within the room. High school students may want to be "cool," but they enjoy doing things that involve teacher interaction. On one round table, I would keep a small jigsaw puzzle for students who arrived early. In a cabinet accessible to students, I kept shoe boxes of pictures from European travels. Magazines and books from foreign travels were available in a bookcase. Not every student got involved, but usually the ones most easily bored and most apt to create problems would be the ones who got involved with the interest areas. Often the student who is the most rowdy will be the one most helpful in a class hands-on project.

In addition to the difficulty of getting the class on track, there is another area of time that presents possible discipline problems. Schools that use a block schedule will have teachers who find it almost impossible to fill all the period with learning activity. Students give testimony to the fact that several teachers will give the last few minutes of class for free time. If the teacher does not provide for the students, the students just may furnish their own entertainment. Teachers in the elementary schools set up interest centers for students to work independently, but this method is not often found in the high school classroom. We have a reading teacher whose room is loaded with interest centers and exploration/individual learning nooks. Other teachers who visit Lisa's room will make such remarks as, "I could live in this room." She has managed to make small cubicles using cheap shower curtains. She has castoff couches, bean bags, small book centers, and lots of growing plants. I have been in her room as a period is closing, and the students remain in some type of learning activity until the bell rings and often have to be prodded out of the room.

The interest centers work better with teacher interaction. The students may want to ask questions or just have a moment to casually chat with the teacher. An interest center works somewhat like a yard sale. Years ago, I participated in rummage sales for charity in a downtown area of Owensboro, Kentucky. If we were sitting, watching the crowd pass by, customers were few, but if we began to refold and rearrange the rummage, people would come into the area to interact about the merchandise. Sales would go up! In the same manner, students will show very little interest in a teacher's collection, but if that teacher begins to talk to a student about the item or picture, a group will soon gather.

One year, I tried an experiment with a special chair that I placed right beside my desk. I told the students that if they had a special need or concern, they could sit in the chair that day and at some point in the period, I would get to their problem. The chair was never empty. In fact, some asked if I would put a chair on the other side of the desk, and I did. Also, it worked well for discipline. If a student was disruptive, I would just pull up another chair and ask that student to join the others. The atmosphere around the teacher's desk created a will to work, and the disruptive student would find himself or herself in guided instruction. This method may never be approved as a way to correct disruptive behavior because the offender may even feel a little privileged rather than punished. Oddly enough, I learned that a student's behavior was generally better after having spent a class period in the special chair.

My thoughts often go back to that resource teacher who voiced that her whole school needed help. My elder son substituted in that school for a few days and found it unbearable. One class was so bad that the substitute coordinator sent the deputy to the classroom to check on him about 15 minutes into the period. How do we help a whole school? Recently, along with four other teachers, I attended a two-day reading strategies workshop in Nashville, Tennessee. At the end of the second day's session, the presenter, Dr. Judith Irwin, asked us to discuss within small groups the methods of implementation of the strategies within our schools. She chose me as the spokesperson for my group and my answer was somewhat flippant, "Change comes into an organization or institution much the same way you move a cemetery—one body at a time." In spite of the comical imagery, there is truth in the statement. I would think that we could help a whole school one classroom at a time. If we can find out what is working for one teacher in that school who has the same students as the teacher down the hall who has chaos, we can begin a plan for improvement. In our district in-house workshop, presenters and mentors are used. Collaboration with a successful peer can often result in sharing strategies that work effectively for other teachers.

Students need guidelines and restrictions. They want to know where the boundaries are. They are comfortable working within a teacher's framework of rules and regulations as long as they are administered with respect. My twin nieces are in the seventh grade in a small school in Tennessee. Before school started this year, they dreaded and complained about a certain teacher who inevitably would appear on their schedule of four teachers. When the school year was half over, their mother reported that she never hears anything about the other three teachers, but "Ms. Wilson" is constantly in the conversation. The girls frequently quote and refer to that one "dreadful" teacher with "Ms. Wilson says . . . ." Surprisingly, the repeated instruction or trivia is all positive. Some of the most loved and honored teachers are the ones who require the most from their students. Of course, there must be an accompanying caring attitude and respect for the student on the part of the teacher.

In the small town of Corbin, Kentucky, at one of the three elementary schools, the fourth grade teacher had a reputation of being difficult. One August, our doorbell rang and on our porch stood a parent of an upcoming fourth grader for that school. She said, "I know that you have a son who will be in the fourth grade this fall, and I'm sure that you would like to sign a petition against Mrs. Smith who is scheduled to be their teacher." We, of course, didn't sign the petition. Before school started, my husband had a conference with Mrs. Smith in regard to our son's reading difficulties. She warned, "Mr. Prewitt, I will work with you on the problem, but you must know that to bring a child from remedial reading to the level of the regular students is almost impossible." That year, Mrs. Smith, along with the help of my husband, brought our son from remedial reading designation into the regular reading group! What if we had signed the petition?

The Latin teacher in our school is strict and requires students to be committed to the task of learning Latin. He expects good attendance and make-up work for absences. He positions his students in the traditional one-behind-the-other seating arrangement. There is no doubt to the visitor in his room that this teacher is unquestionably in charge. He is devoted to the teaching of Latin, and even though his classes are a difficult, academic elective, they always are full with waiting lists. How does this happen? I asked one of his Latin III students why he liked Latin so much. He answered, "I don't like Latin. I like the teacher." I asked, "What about him or his classes make you like him?" He answered, "He makes class fun. We are always doing something different. He tells funny stories."
One of the activities I have observed is toga day. Students make their own costumes and wear them all day from class to class. Another day, I entered his classroom and found all the chairs pushed against the wall, and they were replaced with some type of platform that covered most of the main area of the room. The students had brought Roman food and were lying on the floor in their togas, eating in Roman style. The atmosphere on these special days is that of a secret order meeting on some special assignment. The students feel special and exclusive. The next day, they are back in rows, working diligently on an assignment from the textbook. He has won their respect. They feel privileged to be a part of this class, and they will do whatever is necessary to be in this teacher's good favor.

In my first year of teaching, I had seventh and eighth graders mixed in a type of "at-risk" grouping. Finding it difficult to get and keep their attention, I would resort to raising my voice which seemed to help for the moment. One day, I asked a veteran teacher, who had weathered the storm accompanying racial integration of the schools, what was his secret to a quiet classroom. Perhaps he had passed my room and heard me yelling, but his only answer was, "Always talk in a quiet, calm manner. If you shout at the students, they will wait until you begin shouting to respond." Immediately, I used his advice and found that it was much more effective. Since that time, it has been rare that I have raised my voice in the classroom for the purpose of discipline or call to attention. I also learned by experimentation that students can be trained to fall immediately quiet when I stand behind the lectern and wait for their attention.

As I previously related, after my first year of teaching, I succumbed to discouragement and dropped out. Since I needed some extra money, I began substituting. In this role, observation of the teachers became possible through the behavior of their students. The teachers' management and discipline methods were graphically evident in the students' actions while the teacher was away. I found that teachers who left no seating charts, no roll sheets, and no lesson plans (yes! this happens!) left chaos in the classroom. Students would exemplify behaviors from direct back talk, leaving class without permission, skipping the class altogether when word circulated that there was a substitute, and general disrespect for any effort of order. On the other hand, teachers who left specific directions and plans generally had well-behaved, respectful students.

In my substituting experience, the most extreme case of classroom regimentation presented itself in a junior English class. The teacher was a young, well-built, football-type man named Mr. Little, who was also the cheerleading coach. The assistant principal handed me a sheaf of papers which were the class-by-class instructions, seating charts, and lesson plans. Mr. Little had included a response sheet for me which looked like this:

Period One:

Record names assigned to any seats that are empty _____

_____

If anyone is not sitting in the right seat, do not disturb him/her, but write the name here _____

If anyone talks during the assignment, write the name here _____

If anyone is not working on the assignment, write the name here _____

Please take up all papers by the end of the period. If there has been any difficulty in regard to classroom procedure or behavior, please explain: _____

The form accompanied plans for every period. He included a page that thanked me for my cooperation, and he asked me to sign the sheet. On my way to his room, I read the instructions, and with a smile of amusement, I said to myself, "Yeah! this is going to happen!" But, it did happen! The students filed in quietly, took their seats quietly, responded to roll call and instructions respectfully, did their work diligently, and all sat in the assigned seats. Period after period came and went in the same manner. Last period came, and I could stand the curiosity no longer. I asked a student near the desk to share with me Mr. Little's secret in creating such model behavior in his absence.
The answer was two-fold. One, there would be accountability the next day in regard to what I wrote on that evaluation sheet. Some sort of disciplinary action would result from any infraction. Two, Mr. Little had the reputation of being the best teacher in the English Department, and it was considered a great privilege to be a member of his class. They understood the purpose of their presence in his room, and they rose to meet the challenge.

If procedures, goals, or objectives are not given to the students, they will devise their own action plan. The lack of a plan invites boredom, which will result in misbehavior or inattentiveness to the point of slumber.

Suggestions for Classroom Discipline

1. Invent a procedure to get the students' attention. Purchase Harry Wong's book *The First Days of School* and adopt some of his methods and procedures. If possible, view his video set *The Effective Teacher*.

2. Experiment with various procedures to get the students immediately involved in a learning activity. Some suggestions:

   A. Assign journal writing (you prepare the question and have it on the board or overhead);
   B. Give them some sort of handout (even brain teaser puzzles) as they enter;
   C. Have the day's agenda listed on the board.

3. Create interest centers and interact with students when they show an interest.

4. Interact with students after they have shut down for the day. Sometimes the teacher is the only person who actually listens. Through building a relationship with the student, discipline is more easily achieved.

5. If you make a threat (detention for example), stand behind your word. A law without penalty is of no use.

6. Refuse to talk or attempt to teach over their noise or inattentiveness. Establish methods of obtaining their attention without shouting or competing for the floor.

7. Avoid using humiliation as a discipline tactic. If you can contribute to a child's self-respect, that student will tend to rise to your expectations.

8. An administrator may help with discipline strategies, but students must see the teacher as the disciplinarian. You, as the teacher, are the leader in the classroom and you must be in charge.

Overcoming Obstacles

Existence in a world that has been dictated by tradition, culture, family, or circumstance can often inhibit happiness. In some cultures, the class distinction could cause a person to feel trapped into a certain channel of action or inaction. In other areas, family expectations may cause a person to draft a future plan on a course that is based on the choices made by others. I recall a story of a young man who gave up the girl of his choice because his family members thought she was not the right "type" for him. His mother was adamant in her protests, so he listened to their suggestions and married the girl of their choice. The marriage was doomed for failure and divorce followed. Many years later at a family reunion, family members were discussing past acquaintances when one sister remarked, "Whatever happened to that girl, Mary, that you once liked?" "I don't know," he replied. "She would have made you a good wife," the mother joined in the conversation. "I heard that Mary went to college and is doing well in the business world," another family member contributed. "Why didn't you marry Mary?" the sister innocently asked. The man was speechless! How could they be so thoughtless as to suggest that it were he who had made the wrong choice?

In place of having a scapegoat, others may be suffering from unhappy circumstances resulting from their own poor choices. For several years, each semester I taught one class as an adjunct professor at a community college. At times my assignment consisted of teaching a college prep English class, a remedial course created for those students who lack sufficient skills for entrance into the regular English composition courses. On the first night of a particular semester, a student, arriving a little late, rolled into my room in a wheelchair. She seemed a little aggressive in locating a suitable table at which to park her chair, but I attributed her actions to embarrassment or discomfort in her situation. She looked frightened, yet very determined. I learned from the roll sheets that her name was Rusty.

Rusty stayed for a chat after class and informed me that she was a prisoner who was being escorted to and from class by correctional officers. She was scheduled for release in the near future, and it was recommended by her counselors and case workers that she enroll in some type of job rehabilitation program since she had been incarcerated for 12 years. She opted to go to college for a computer science associates degree. Not having rubbed shoulders with the "outside" for 12 years, Rusty was indeed frightened and unsure.

Confiding that she was 50 years old, Rusty explained her fears of college. "I don't know what I'm doing," she said. "I just passed the GED test and now I'm enrolled in 12 hours, and I don't even know what college is all about. I haven't been in a classroom for many years." Seeing her obvious terror, I chatted for awhile and attempted to reassure her. I pointed out that going to school was like eating a big dinner. We start with the appetizer and go through the rest, course by course. She was looking at the whole layout and was feeling like a dinner guest that wasn't sure which fork to use.

Rusty then asked me if I was afraid to have her in my class. A little puzzled, I simply answered, "No." She went on to explain that another teacher, whose class had already met, had requested Rusty to be dropped from her class roll because she was uneasy with prison-related students. More shocking to me was the nature of the course that was replaced. Rusty told me that the fear-ridden teacher taught mental health! What a paradox! It is difficult for me to comprehend the teacher's reluctance to meet the challenge of dealing with an exceptional student.

Quickly, I reassured Rusty that I was not afraid of her. In fact, I shared with her that my husband and I had opened our home as an emergency shelter for delinquent teenage boys for six years. "Rusty," I said, "I have lived with many criminals ranging from crimes of truancy to murder, so I have no reservations concerning our classroom association." Greatly relieved, she smiled broadly and replied, "Oh, good! You understand." Indeed, I did and I reassured her that our relationship began the moment that she rolled into the classroom and anything beforehand was irrelevant.

Before we left that night, Rusty was smiling and joking about her situation. "What happened to Chevrolets, Fords, and Cadillacs?" she asked. I don't recognize any of these little cars." Surveying the parking lot after class, I tried to see through Rusty's eyes, and I saw what looked like compact city of little cars looking almost as though they came from a clone factory.

As the semester progressed, I saw a change in Rusty. She was becoming more confident, and obviously she was enjoying her release time from the prison. Other students made her welcome, and one or two actually reached out in friendship. Her boundaries were expanding, and it was obvious from the smile on her face that she was making big deposits into her happiness account. My last remembrance of Rusty is an image of her and several students studying, snacking, and conversing in the student union.

We have to be alert and look for those small openings that lead us out of our restrictive circumstance whatever it may be. I'm sure that we have all felt trapped, but that is not the time to lie down and wallow in our misfortunes. The temptation to enjoy our misery is universal. Generally speaking, those people who have suffered loss of love are those who play the "somebody's done somebody wrong" songs. The old saying, "Misery loves company," could be changed to "Misery loves miserable company." As long as we enjoy the misery, we will not find the way out.

Holes in the barriers which restrict happiness can be found in most every situation. When my elder son, Billy, entered the first grade, he prided himself on being a fast runner. Of course, he could outrun his brother who was two years younger, but Billy also could outrun other kids in the neighborhood. Recess activities at school became racing events, but Billy had met one who was his match and more. One day, Billy came home beaming with good news. He had discovered his problem! He needed new shoes—a certain kind of shoe! "Mom," he informed me persuasively, "if I just had new shoes, I could outrun Scott."

Be it far from this mother to let a little thing like new shoes stand in the way of her son's becoming number one! That evening the shoes were purchased. Of course, I didn't believe for one minute in the shoes, but I did believe in my son's perception of the problem and its solution. I anxiously waited for the next day's racing results. "Mom," he reported, "I didn't win, but I was closer. I just need to break in my new shoes. I'll win tomorrow." He was glowing with the feeling of success, yet he had lost! Sure enough, the next day and most days thereafter, he was the number one runner at recess.

Was it the shoes? Would he have won without them? The person who achieves happiness doesn't stop when encountering the problem; instead, a way out of the dilemma is sought. All teachers can relate stories of students who overcame great obstacles to their performance in the classroom. The gamut may run from lack of proper sleep and nourishment to problems as extreme as drugs and alcoholism. One of my former students in English II had an extreme behavior change. He went from an alert, cheerful, and on-task student to one who showed no interest. He lapsed into apathy and his lethargy resulted in napping in the classroom. Admittedly, I know that English II is not the greatest motivational subject on the schedule, but his problem reached beyond that of mere boredom. James had a problem that needed intervention. I asked James about his sleepiness, but the answer was guarded.

Finally, one morning he came in and lay on the floor before roll call. When it came time for class, I could not get him awake! He slept the whole class period! It was time to call the father. Fortunately, his problem was simple. He had started a job at a local restaurant, and the last few days, he had been closing the restaurant. Of course, he didn't want to tell me because the restaurant was violating the child labor laws in keeping him until 11:00 or midnight. The father had a talk with the restaurant's manager, and things smoothed out. James was back on-task. In cases of this type, the teacher seems to become the guardian or at least a trouble-shooter for the child.

Also, teachers may have their own assortment of personal problems that inhibit happiness in or out of the classroom. A "floating" teacher was assigned into my classroom for the first period of the day. I knew that he had been on a leave of absence for alcohol rehabilitation, but he had stabilized enough to resume classroom duty. Over the year, we developed a camaraderie sufficient enough for him to talk of his addiction. Over and over, he would assure me that he had control of the situation. I don't know what happened during the summer, but as school progressed the next fall, rumors began to surface that he was not doing well. Students began to report that he smelled of alcohol in the classroom. Finally, one morning, he came to the classroom more than a little inebriated. Students came to the office for help, and the teacher was put on immediate suspension.

Out of concern and remembered pleasant conversations the previous year, I called to offer any assistance I could give. Understandably, he was devastated and unable to talk. A couple of weeks later, I called again. This time, he was able to talk about the seriousness of his situation. He needed a job. The last time I called, he was jovial and informed me that he had enrolled in some computer classes and was looking forward to a career change. Apparently, he recognized his need for rerouting his energies and overcoming the obstacle. At least, he was actively pursuing a hole in his fence of entrapment.

We have all heard the statement, "I've fallen and I can't get up." The statement is intended to be humorous because most often it is quoted at a time that is intended to bring a smile or a laugh. A professor colleague of mine gave me his version of the statement: "I've fallen, and I can't reach my beer." Whatever version we want to use, the mental picture is the same. We see ourselves lying flat (maybe even in a fetal position) on the floor, lifeless, useless, helpless, seemingly stripped of all energies or abilities or assistance that would help us to our feet. I mentally picture a cockroach that turns on his back to die. I even tried to help one of these creatures get back on his feet by turning him right side up, but he managed to turn back over to continue his death struggle. So, I left him alone to die in his own way.

How do we fall to such a position in our self-concept? Perhaps someone or some circumstance has just thrown us a curve ball, we struck out, and the crowd booed us to the dugout where we sit and lick our injured self-pride. Does that mean we will never take the bat again when the umpire announces, "Batter up"? Of course not. Even Babe Ruth, who for many years held the record for the most home runs in a season, struck out more times than he made hits. Hopefully, our fallen state is a temporary condition, but at the time, the blow may appear to be fatal to our self-image. Passing the blame may help us a little, but eventually we must face ourselves. Flip Wilson's phrase, "The devil made me do it" is a little saying that appeared for awhile on T-shirts, baby clothing, and other applicable places. The statement is humorous and may contain an element of truth, but happiness lies in facing our actions and rerouting the course.

Life is full of bullets or blows that may knock us flat or at least to our knees. The getting up is our responsibility. A helping hand is always appreciated, but most of the time we have to shake ourselves, survey the situation, and pull ourselves up above the floor level. People speak with admiration in regard to those people who have "pulled themselves up by their own boot straps." One contributing factor to our crash landing may be the mistake of allowing others to act as judge and jury over us. If we delegate that kind of power, it most likely will be accepted by others, and there are always those who will volunteer to be our navigator while others will serve as our judge and jury. The beginning teachers may be more vulnerable in that they are usually given the worst classrooms and the worst assignments. If there is a material shortage, the new teacher is usually the one without supplies or textbooks or whatever is short. They do not have the knowledge of the school to enable them to find what they need in old closets or someone else's room. A feeling of being shortchanged or looked over can create a self-image of a lesser citizen of the teaching community. The creation of a support group and mentors among the beginning teachers and those new to the school can greatly relieve these anxieties.

A humorous portrayal of the concept of getting knocked down surfaced in a film called *Kindergarten Cop* starring Arnold Swartzenegger. To get his criminal, the character went undercover as a kindergarten teacher. After the first day in the classroom, the cop, turned teacher, was exhausted because the children had absolutely taken over. They dictated the day in very aggressive behaviors. The poor cop was beaten, floored, and stumped for a clue on how he was to coexist with the little monsters who had taken charge of his life. Of course, a beautiful coworker came to the rescue and gave him instructions of how he was to "take charge." The next day, we saw the great cop apply the military system to that little class of youngsters and by midmorning, he was in charge.

Someone is going to be in charge of our lives, and we hold the power in our hands to select whether it will be ourselves or whether we will relinquish the controls to another. From the time we are born until we die, there are always those powers-that-be that dictate our moves. How can we keep from getting trampled?

A woman of questionable reputation attended our church sporadically. One night she called me from the local county jail. She had been charged with a misdemeanor and had been sentenced to 30 days in jail. For the next 30 minutes, she gave a running monologue of all her woes inside and outside the prison. I politely listened, but obviously there was nothing else I could do. I hung up emotionally drained. A few nights later, she called again and spent 45 minutes of my time rehearsing the same complaints. That time, I was so drained that I took my complaint to my husband. His simple answer was, "The next time she calls, just tell her that you can't engage in being a listening service. You are the one who is allowing her to dump the garbage." I went for sympathy and I got directions for garbage elimination!

The next time she called, I followed through on the instructions. For a few seconds, the line was silent. The silence was followed with a general chewing out aided by the use of some words that she did not learn in church. Perhaps I added to her happiness because she had one more item and person to add to her already long list of personal offenders. Of course, she did not call again, and I had eliminated a negative drain by taking control. One motivational speaker went as far as to say, "Get rid of all negative influences in your life, and for some, that may even be a divorce." Surely, he was exaggerating to get his point across, but often we may have to dissolve a friendship in order to get rid of the negativism that inhibits happiness.

77

Most of us will find a way to evade that person who is looking for a garbage dump, but what about that person who is out to give us a make-over? Associates may unknowingly give us a put-down feeling just because they are trying to constructively improve us. One of my cousins related an incident from his teenage years. He would write to an uncle who lived at a great distance from him. That uncle would return the nephew's letter with all the grammar errors circled and corrected. Rather than helping the boy learn grammar, the nephew began to feel fearful of the uncle and the letters became fewer. As teachers, we may feel intimidated by those teachers who appear to have greater expertise in communication skills, but that does not make us second-rate teachers.

Many years ago when I was a teenager, my father showed me a small anecdote from the *Reader's Digest*. If my father were trying to teach me a lesson to help me in my know-it-all years, at the very least, the lesson was successful in that I remember it to this day when I find myself sounding critical. A young teacher was invited to a luncheon and sat next to an elderly, retired English teacher. Wanting to make a good impression, the younger teacher made corrections a couple of times when someone made a grammar error in conversational speaking. Later, she asked the retiree, "Doesn't it bother you when people use the language so carelessly? Why don't you speak up and let people know when they are in error?" The elderly teacher replied, "My dear, I believe that good manners are better than good English."

On the other hand, our perception of or reaction to a particular circumstance or situation may become an obstacle to happiness. As a teenager, I needed braces to correct an overbite. "Bucky" was not my idea of a great nickname. I asked my dentist about braces, and he told me that my problem was bone structure and could not be fixed by braces. "Besides that," he said, "someone would have to drive you to Middlesboro once a month for adjustments." Middlesboro was 50 miles away over winding roads, and my dad would have to take off work without pay. Accepting his verdict, I lived with my unhappiness and learned to compensate somewhat by consciously dropping my lower jaw.

Over the years, students enjoyed finding subtle ways of making fun of my overbite. The most classic example happened while I was substituting in a middle school. Students returned from lunch and laid carrots on my desk. I thanked them and went on. Not satisfied, one of the girls raised her hand and asked me if I were from Beaver Dam which is a small town just south of Owensboro, Kentucky, where I then lived. Now, I was used to the metaphor of the rabbit, but the "beaver" was a new one. It actually slid right past my recognition, and I innocently stated that, "No, I am from a little town in the foothills of the Appalachian Mountains." My answer was so sincere that no one laughed and there were no more questions. It was only after I got home that I understood the intentional pun.

Several years later, when we moved back to my hometown, the small township had been blessed by the arrival of two orthodontists, who had recently set up office. One afternoon, I was hosting a ladies' luncheon at the local cafeteria when I was called aside by a former high school teacher who wanted to introduce me to his luncheon companion. "Arlene," he said, "I want you to meet Dr. Ray Smith, who is an orthodontist." I would rather have met a famous hairdresser on a bad hair day! I lost my smile immediately and managed to stumble through the introduction. Dr. Smith smiled kindly it seemed, but I felt totally undressed, stripped naked. Weakly, I hurried away, making excuses that I needed to get back to the luncheon.

Putting Dr. Smith out of mind wasn't difficult because I had been living in denial for years. But, a few days later while reading one of Dr. Robert Schuller's books, I came across a statement that spoke directly to me. As an example, he used someone who needed nose surgery. In summary, his statement gave me the message: "If you have what you think is a physical defect, and it can be fixed, get up immediately and start the process to get something done." I arose and looked up the number of Dr. Smith and called immediately for a consultation appointment. Between the time of the call and the actual appointment, I lived with a lot of misgivings. The time arrived, and I was scared and embarrassed. How could a 34-year-old woman walk into a waiting room filled with teenagers? I tucked Dr. Schuller's book into my purse for courage.

When Dr. Smith entered the little conference room, he recognized me and greeted me warmly. I told him why I came and explained why I had not been fitted for braces at an earlier time. I was expecting him to say, "Yes, I agree. Your problem is one of bone structure." On the contrary, he ignored my excuses and continued to fill out a form on the table in front of him. "Who referred you?" he asked. I guess he was waiting for the name of a local dentist. Not knowing what to say, I replied, "Dr. Robert Schuller." His pen stopped in midair, and I knew I had to give an explanation. Pulling the book from my purse, I confessed, "Dr. Schuller told me in this book to get my mouth fixed." He smiled, but he left that part of the questionnaire blank. He wasn't quite sure how to handle this situation because it seemed that I was his first patient who just walked in off the street. There was no "Drop-ins Welcome" sign in the window.

I got my braces and felt happier and prettier immediately. I may not have a million-dollar smile, but I've made a big investment toward it. One young man in our church complimented me by saying, "You should wear braces always. Your smile is beautiful and you look younger." WOW! That 34-year-old woman was walking on a cloud of happiness. The problem was far from fixed but the solution was on the way. One immediate outcome was that I no longer felt like I had buckteeth and was never again ridiculed for my overbite. Initially, with the braces the defect was even more accented, especially after losing two teeth to make space for the gradual backward movement of the teeth. Just the fact that I was actively working on the problem gave me confidence to smile anyway.

If we will internalize the statement that no one can insult us, if we believe it and start applying it, some changes will be made in our concepts. The martyr attitude, which some people find so attractive, will have to make an exit. Self-pity must leave the stage as we make the switch from "That person just flattened me," to "That person just attempted to insult me." If we are unwilling to turn loose of our "I've been mistreated" approach, then we will have indeed fallen, and we can't get up!

In the fall of 1996, I made a trip to Corbin, Kentucky, with the purpose of finding people who had known Colonel Harland Sanders. The owners of an old furniture store across the street from his original establishment directed me to a beauty salon a few yards away that was owned by the Colonel's niece. The hairdressers were reluctant to talk and called the niece who graciously agreed to make an appearance to be interviewed. While talking to the niece, an unnoticed elderly lady under a hair dryer peered out from under the dome of the dryer and said, "I used to work for Colonel Sanders when I was young." Excitement flowed through me because I knew that she would have the stories I wanted.

Before Colonel Sanders became famous, he ran into an obstacle that sent him into years of research. Sanders Restaurant and Court in Corbin, Kentucky, was strategically located at the intersection of Highway 25 and 25E. At that time, Highway 25 was the main artery of transportation from Michigan to Florida. Plans were being made to build an interstate highway (I-75) that would bypass Sanders Court and Restaurant by several miles. The new road could wipe out the tourist trade for the little town. Colonel Sanders didn't wait for the road. He began experimenting with recipes for chicken and methods of preparation.

The former waitress told me of his several years of working in a little screened-in kitchen in the back of the restaurant where he eventually developed the pressure frying method along with his "secret recipe." She was very proud of the fact that she had been one of his tasters. After developing his recipe, he needed advertisement. Undaunted, he would load his white Cadillac with the pressure fryer and bags of his recipe and would head out to a restaurant, any restaurant. Upon arriving, he would tell the manager/owner that he wanted to cook the chicken that day, and he would spend the day in the kitchen. At the end of the day, he would have made a sale for his franchise. And the rest is history.

The escape routes exist in the fences, but it is up to us to find them. It is rare that someone will actually hand us the solution to a problem. Some teachers know that they are failing in effectiveness, but they may not have the awareness or willingness to research ways to overcome their weaknesses. One teacher tiredly expressed, "I don't know how much longer I can manage kids. I just hope I can hold out to retirement." Obstacles are sometimes tolerated because we feel comfortable with our assumed limitations, or we may just feel embarrassed to admit that we need help. Acceptance or denial means that we are exempt from doing any explaining to anyone and most of all to ourselves. We eat, sleep, work, and start all over again, but are we happy?

Let me be quick to recognize that sometimes people fall and there is no getting up. There are no cures, no answers. A famous British poet, John Keats, died at age 26 with tuberculosis. One of his greatest regrets after he learned he was dying was that he would die with much of his poetry still in him. He did not have enough time to share his poetry with the world. During a visit to Rome, Italy, I spent some time at the John Keats Memorial that has been established in the apartment where he died. While there, I read some of his original letters and manuscripts. The pain of his mortality is evident in his writings. Three years before his death, Keats began one of his sonnets with the lines, "When I have fears that I may cease to be / Before my pen has gleaned my teeming brain." Two years before his death, he wrote another sonnet that began, "Bright star! would I were steadfast as thou art—." He had fallen, and even though he used every available means to get up, he succumbed to his illness.

While we have options, let us reach for that helping hand, that tidbit of hope. We may have to ignore the would-be consoler who dumps negative thoughts into our condition, and we may find that overcoming negativism is the biggest part of the battle.

Suggestions for Overcoming Obstacles

1. As the teacher, you may be the key in helping that student overcome difficult situations. Identify the students with the most difficult situations and be as pleasant as possible to the exceptional students. Loving the unlovable may take twice the effort, but the rewards could be outstanding.

2. Allow yourself the indulgence of receiving help. Many times when we have fallen or have a need, there is a hand offered to lift us up. In our unhappiness, we may be blinded to the help or even refuse to allow others to share in our troubles. If we will be open, we will find our happiness in the give and take of sharing during the times of sorrow or trouble.

3. If it is a fixable obstacle, begin steps in the direction of its resolution. I knew a lady who would sit the vacuum cleaner in the middle of the living room when she needed to clean house but had other things she wanted to do. The symbol of the vacuum cleaner made her feel as though she was aware of the problem and at least had it on the agenda.

4. Internalize the statement that no one can insult you without your permission. Retaliation may give an immediate power surge, but the energy will soon dissipate. Sharpening the ability to reject the insult or snide remark will develop strength of character. Addressing every little remark made by a student will take up valuable time and will not foster a learning environment.

5. Practice thinking positive thoughts about yourself and sharing positive feedback to others.

Conquering Fears

I'm sure we have all worried about things that never happened the way we had imagined in our fear. We aren't sure of the source or the reason why we got into such a fearful state of mind; therefore, we are susceptible to a recurrence of the same type of fear. By examining our fears in a rational manner while we are comfortable, perhaps we can find some ways in which to reduce or eliminate these happiness-robbing practices.

I've been told that the only fears that we are born with are the fear of falling and the fear of loud noises. If that is so, I managed to do a lot of accumulated learning in my early years because I seemed to have piled up many fears in my emotional system. For example, why do I keep a dress in the closet that I do not like? Answer: fear of being unable to replace it. I listened to a tape by one speaker who advised that we should get rid of all clothes in our closet that we haven't worn for a year or that we had negative feelings about. Following such advice is a little different from the mental trash can beside the bed. This exercise was for real, and it involved tangible property. Nevertheless, in spite of my misgivings, I followed his advice, hoping to rid myself of negative influences. Afterward, I had a lot of room in my closet, and the cleansing did give a pleasant feeling. On the other hand, I enjoy throwing things away, so I wasn't sure from which activity I was getting the positive input.

Our fears may spring from the feelings of uselessness. We may compensate by busying ourselves in order to feel secure of our place in the scheme of the universe. One of my high school juniors remained after class to ask me about happiness. He said, "Mrs. Prewitt, I don't know how to know if I'm happy. I know that I like it when I'm very busy, and I always go from one project directly to another, sometimes spending lots of time on extra-curricular activities. I worry about getting it all done, but when I get it all finished, I start worrying because I am not worried about something! I start looking for something else to worry about." He continued, "If I have nothing to do, I absolutely crash, and I want to do nothing. My mind goes dead, and I forget to do the small routine things. At that time, I don't feel very happy."

He could have been describing me! Actually, he looked a little relieved when I told him so. I helped him examine his feelings. "Ben, do you suppose that being busy makes you happy because you feel needed and worthwhile?"

"Maybe," he smiled. Knowing that he worked on the school launch team which involved the building and launching of scale shuttles (NASA even sent officials to monitor their launches), I asked him if his worrying when he was not busy could be a type of "postpartum blues" because, all of a sudden, with one thrust of power, the long awaited day has come and gone.

His smile and "maybe" came again.

"Ben," I said, "most likely you are finding happiness in the feelings of productivity, the feeling of being useful and needed. When you are busy, it gives your life purpose and direction." "That may be it, Mrs. Prewitt," he said. "Thanks," and with a smile he was out the door.

Fear of being unable to produce can cripple us in the workplace. We are afraid to apply for a promotion or to teach a different grade level or skill level. "What if I get turned down?" we ask ourselves. "Everyone will know that I was considered inadequate," we think. Feeling that it is safer to remain where we are, we do nothing and are later forced to watch a colleague, maybe with lesser abilities, take the coveted position. Are we justified in our complaints? No! But we tend to indulge in complaining; and, as a result, dissatisfaction and resentment very likely will come to dwell with us.

How often have we thought, "I would like to change jobs," but some sort of fear kept us from filling out the application. We all have those discontented days on our jobs. One country music singer, Charlie Pride, made a hit song by saying what many wish to say out loud, "You can take this job and shove it!" With every decision that we make to remain passive, we are rejecting ourselves; therefore, our brain computes the unhappy word *failure*. Rather than face the fear of advancement, we may find ourselves stuck in our comfort zone.

I once knew a man in his thirties who had studied and earned a degree in agriculture from Berea College, a college in Kentucky noted for its program of educating the Kentucky students through working scholarships. He loved the idea of being a county agricultural agent, and he had the educational qualifications. He was employed in a greeting card factory and earned an adequate income, but on occasions he would bring a clipping from the want-ad section of the newspaper and show it to my husband. It was always the same. One of the counties in that tri-county area was advertising for a county agriculture agent.

My husband would encourage him to prepare a resumé and to apply for the position. He would even offer to assist him in the preparation and offered himself as a reference. The young man never once submitted his application. Why? What was he afraid of? Was he afraid of rejection? Was he afraid he might get hired and then couldn't do the job? My guess is that he had a barrier of fear built so tall that he couldn't see over it and was paralyzed.

Perhaps there are times that we reverse the coin, and we actually fear success. We ask, "What if I get the promotion; can I do the job?" My sister, Judy, once worked long and hard hours preparing a job resumé and cover letter that would usher her from hourly wage to a salaried position. Learning that she had to meet an interview committee and make an oral presentation, she did more research and consulted me to help in the structure of her preparation. She did get the job, but immediately she called with another concern. "I have the job, but what if I can't perform the task?" I reassured her that a whole committee had screened her and assessed her as the best. However, if she had fixed her eyes on the magnitude of the responsibility before she even applied, perhaps fear would have overtaken her spirit and doomed her to the hourly position. Let's not be guilty of looking ahead to the "what ifs" and allowing the idea of being in a new position to frighten us to the point that we never take the first step.

On a more simple level, fear can keep us from trying a new method or an innovative idea in our classroom. We are comfortable with the methods and plans that we have used. What if the new idea doesn't work and we lose control? Fear of change is unsettling when the administration hands us a mandate that must be met. For example, school systems are in the process of eliminating all paperwork. Attendance and grades can be reported directly through the computer to the processing center. Teachers who are susceptible to unfounded fears will panic when the deadlines arrive. They attend training after training and go back to their rooms and keep using the old method. At the same time, there is that nagging stress that whispers, "This is not going to go away." Usually, when the time comes for them to actually employ the knowledge, they wonder why it took so long to make that step, and they are very proud of their accomplishments.

My biggest job stress comes when I am asked to do something that I am not sure I have the knowledge and background to successfully complete. I don't mind the work; it is the dread of facing the challenge or an obstacle that causes the stress. Once I have clear-cut directions and understand them, I actually feel the stress drain away. Surely this principle applies to the student if we give unclear directions or assignments. The directions may be clear to us, but we aren't the ones doing the work.

My sister received her master's degree at age 40, and she proudly invited me to her graduation. Usually, the most boring part of the graduation (unless there is an excessive number of graduates) is the speech given by a distinguished administrator or an invited speaker. It wasn't long into the speech when I realized that this man, Stephen Ranken Weisz, M. Div., Ed. D., had something to say. His speech was titled "When There Is No Map," and he entranced the audience with stories of people who "marched off the map." After the ceremony, my sister and I approached Dr. Weisz to compliment him on the speech. I stated that I had tried to take notes, and he immediately said, "If you want a copy of my speech, just walk with me to my office, and I will give you one." This busy administrator in all his graduation regalia, walked with us across the campus to his office and made copies of his speech! Now I was more impressed with him than with his speech!

From Dr. Weisz's speech, I would like to quote this passage: "Harold Lamb in his biography of Alexander the Great has pointed to the confusion and dismay which came upon the Greek army following Alexander across Asia Minor when they discovered that they had marched right off the map. The only maps they had were Greek which showed only a portion of Asia Minor . . . the rest was blank space. They were confronted, Lamb writes, with the Himalayas, with no directions into what lay beyond." As teachers, we are given workshops, journals, and true-to-life accounts of how things can be improved upon, but often we are afraid to try our own ideas. We need to have the courage to "march off the map" in our area. How many times have we sat in a workshop or read a book that introduced some strategy that is working for someone else and reflected, "I've thought of doing that, but I was afraid it wouldn't work." Someone else had marched off the map at the very place where we had drawn the boundaries.

Dr. Weisz went on to challenge the graduating class. Passionately, he urged, "I hope that none of you will feel satisfied with where you are no matter how intellectually informed you have become here. It is critical that we not remain entrenched in what we already know. In order to respond to the moral and ethical issues of our times, we must all continue to expand our thinking. And, so, I would urge you to take advantage of everything that comes your way to expand your mind and spirit." He went on to inform them that to remain safe and secure in one's little world will lessen the achievements and contributions to the society as a whole.

Fear of stepping into the unknown keeps many of us grounded, yet, stepping into an area where we relinquish control may also be a source of fear. A simple and perhaps humorous example of combining the known with the unknown is that day when we first slip into the passenger's seat of the car and hand the keys to that teenage son or daughter. We breathe a big sigh of relief, and we genuinely congratulate that child who finally passes the driver's license test. I had the experience of compounding the "look who's driving the car" fear with "look who's flying the plane." The adventure became unavoidable if I were to remain the loving, supportive mother. My son returned from Kentucky after the first summer in which he earned his private pilot's license. Dad went flying with him right away, but I always had an excuse. Finally, the excuses ran out, and my day in the air came.

Imagine this sane and reasonable woman walking out of the airport with a 17-year-old pilot to put her life into his hands. When I gave him the car keys, I knew that I could tell him how to drive and even take the wheel away if the tension became unbearable. I had no such backup in that little Cessna 150. None of the dials made sense, and the steering gear was so close that I had to consciously avoid it. "Can I just push this thing over out of my way?" I innocently asked. Grinning, my son assured me that it was there in case I needed to fly the plane. Right!

As we were doing the taxi part that would take us to the runway, David casually informed me of my rights, which were none. "Mom," he said. "I'm really glad you are flying with me today, but the first time that you start telling me what to do, I plan to land on the next runway and call Dad and tell him where to pick you up." With that warning, we lumbered down the runway and soared into the air. I was afraid to look out the window. I had flown on the big jets, but I felt as though we were riding around in the air in a very small, uncomfortable car. All the little jolts were frightening, and my stomach felt a little queasy. I did manage to say, "Whatever you do, just keep it as level as possible; I'm not interested in seeing what this plane will do or to what level of expertise you have attained."

When we returned to the Orlando Executive Airport, I felt a little sick; but my happiness level was soaring. I had overcome a major fear and had made my son happy. Sometimes, we just have to make the decision to admit our fear and step out anyway.

A very common fear is the fear of other people, both known and unknown. In an effort to reassure us, one country singer reminded us that "a stranger is just a friend you haven't met." Most of our fears of other people are based on what we assume they are thinking of us and of our actions. How many times have we altered a behavior pattern because the thought entered our brain, "What will 'they' (or 'he' or 'she') think?" Then, if we succumbed to the fear, we tried to mold our behavior to match our interpretation of what their perception of us may be.

Recently, I attended a workshop for enhancement of leadership skills in the area of presentations. The speaker put statistics on an overhead that pinpointed people's top ten fears, and the one that topped the list is fear of speaking before an audience. I suppose this fear rests on other fears of nonacceptance or rejection or criticism. Speakers generally want to hear some type of positive feedback that satisfies the need for validation. My fears have surfaced in dreams where I would find myself standing in front of an audience inadequately dressed or not even dressed at all! Audience participants can perceive a speaker as self-assured, confident, and fully expert because a speaker is generally at his or her best during the presentation. The fearful person may not be able to look further and see that the speaker has traveled that road of fear, but he or she has been willing to "march off the map" and risk rejection in order to make the presentation.

A young lady once expressed to me her fear of eating in a fancy restaurant. She much preferred to call in pizza or eat at a fast-food place. I encouraged her to tell me why. Her reply was, "I'm afraid people are watching me, and I'll do something wrong." Trying to help her, I asked, "When you go to a restaurant, do you watch others eat?" "No," she replied. "Why?" I asked. She replied, "I'm making sure I do the proper things." "That's exactly how much attention they are paying you," I told her. "They are watching you just as intently as you are watching them." She laughed somewhat relieved. "I never thought of it like that."

A teacher friend confessed to me that she was experiencing difficulty in meeting new people after being transferred to another school. Her reason was that she could never think of anything to say that would spark the initial conversation, so she said nothing. She feared that the other person would show a lack of interest and she would feel rejected. She would always wait for people to come to her, and even when approached, her fear was so great that people often thought her snobbish, and the fact that she is physically attractive added to the stereotypical idea of snobbery. She would answer their questions in clipped replies, which discouraged the would-be friend. Later, she felt guilty and ashamed for her lack of involvement in the conversation. Nevertheless, she continued to withdraw from social gatherings and eventually failed to attend department and faculty meetings. She would sit alone in her room and eat granola bars for lunch.

I suggested that she select a co-worker to get acquainted with and to begin with a smile. If the smile were returned, the next day she was to give a greeting. She was so hungry for friendship that she gave it a try. It wasn't long until she had made a new friend. Her loneliness level plummeted and her happiness level leaped.

Fear of other people will stop us before our toes ever cross the starting line. Our poetry will never be recited; our song will never be sung; our speech will never be made; our potential will never be realized. Remember, the person who criticizes is doing less. The heckler is merely a part of the unknown crowd of ticket holders. The players make the mistakes, but they are the ones who score the points. No one's happiness in the stadium will match the happiness of those who cross the finish line.

Suggestions for Elimination of Fears

1. When you feel a reluctance to participate in an activity that would be self-fulfilling, analyze your hesitation. If the culprit is fear, apply a reasoning process to understand the nature of the inhibiting emotion. Make a conscious effort to identify and override the fear and cross the barrier.

2. If you wish to join a particular group at lunch or at another collective function but fear you will not fit, do a little research. What are the interests of the group? One friend took golf lessons just to be able to understand the conversation of her peers. Be open to expanding your knowledge.

3. Focus on the other people of the group. If you make a mistake, they will remember it much less than you do. A University of Florida music professor, who was directing the Florida All State Band, reminded the performers, "Do not dwell on your mistakes. When the concert is over, the audience will remember the beautiful parts. I never lose sleep over mistakes." Most casual groups are just enjoying the camaraderie of the moment and present no threats.

4. Try a new idea or approach or method in the classroom. If it doesn't work, you may create an adaptation that enhances the interest level for you and the students.

5. Do not allow the fear of failure to cripple innovative ideas. Trial and error has always been the school for great ideas.

6. As you overcome small fears and inhibitions, you will find yourself more equipped to overcome larger fears. Most maps of progress are charted in small increments. Rejoice in an accomplishment.

7. Imagine the "worst case scenario." What is the worst thing that can happen as a result of this action? Accept the consequences of the decision and take the leap.

The Pursuit of Happiness

The Constitution of the United States sets forth the precept that all men are "endowed by their Creator with certain unalienable Rights, that among these are Life, Liberty, and the pursuit of Happiness." If we were to have a "man/woman-on-the-street" interview and ask the question, "What do you want from life?" many would answer, "Happiness," yet very few could define what it is they want or how to engage in the "pursuit of happiness."

A person's definition of happiness will depend upon the expectation from life. Some people constantly search for what they think of as happiness, but in reality, they may fail to recognize happiness if it knocked at the door. They may perceive others as having obtained happiness, so they try to chart their course by someone else's map. These people are those who are referred to as trying to "keep up with the Joneses." We can't keep up! By the time we finally get that new riding mower, Mr. Jones has hired a landscape artist!

That same kind of dissatisfaction can spread into all areas of living. We can expect our children to achieve what others achieve. We may show disappointment for a "C" on the report card because we wanted to have a bumper sticker that reads, "My child is an honor student at Brain Elementary." Our naked bumper is a reproach to our child-rearing techniques. One afternoon, I stopped for a light and observed a bumper sticker on a pick-up truck in front of me. It read, "My child beat up your honor student." I couldn't help but smile at the humorous effort to fight back.

Some people may find their happiness in charting a course that is away from the regular, well-traveled avenues of life. To quote Henry David Thoreau, they march to the "beat of a different drummer." I understand that someone tried to "rescue" David Livingston, the medical missionary, from his life of service in Africa. News had leaked that he was very ill, but the great man refused to be "rescued." He had found fulfillment in what most of us would see as a miserable existence.

I read that Mother Teresa gave ice cream to the dying patients who populated her mission in Calcutta, India. When asked why, she replied, "Ice cream is something they have never experienced. I want them to have that moment of happiness before dying." While a bite of ice cream may bring happiness for one, another's happiness may be found in a different treasure. Most of us will agree that happiness does not come with the accumulation of things or money.

The story of Albert Schweitzer, who had played the great grand piano in concert at Carnegie Hall, tells how he received his happiness while relaxing from a day's work in his ill-provisioned, derelict, and leper-populated hospital in French Equatorial Africa. He traded the opportunity of playing the grand piano for thousands of appreciative fans to playing tunes on an old rundown pump organ to an audience of very ill and dying patients. He determined his own happiness. Other factors may determine the record of our existence as "success" or "failure," but we control the decision to be happy.

While I was in graduate school, I became friends with a young lady who thought that having more possessions and prestige created happiness. She visited me one Saturday to share the news that her husband had joined in a business partnership in our small town, and she would soon be moving. The purpose of her visit was to get information about the small town in which I lived. She admitted right at the first that she planned to enter the "upper crust" of that town's society. Having never really considered this little hometown of mine as having an "upper crust," I had to do some thinking.

A sampling of her questions ran like this: "What area of housing is most prestigious?" "Where do the elite attend church?" "What dress shop is considered the most sophisticated?" After some consideration, I concluded that our town had two upper crusts. We had the charter members with their descendants, and we had the newcomers who had formed their own level of crust. I explained as best I could the distinctions, and she made the wise decision to join the newcomers.

I saw her a few times after that, and she happily reported that she was socially climbing, but one day in a weak moment, she admitted that her possessions were sometimes a weight around her neck. She confessed that she was unhappy and wished they could move to Lexington, Kentucky, where life could give her the culture she desired. She added that her mother wanted her to have a child, but she felt that a child would not fit into her life as a socialite.

Not much time elapsed until my friend called with the news that her husband had bought into a partnership in Lexington. She was again filled with great expectations of circulating in high society. If I had a crystal ball which could reveal the future, I'm sure the message would read, "Jennifer's name fails to be listed on Lexington's society registers. The 'crust' tends to be rather elusive to newcomers. Suffering much disappointment, Jennifer is now studying maps for relocation purposes."

I read an interview a few years ago of one of the world's richest men. When asked what it took to make him happy, he replied, "More." But, I wonder, when does "more" become "enough"? People who actively chase happiness may find that it constantly eludes them. They may die feeling that life has been unfair. They never learn the lesson that happiness does not ride on possessions, social standing, or even on success.

On the other hand, we might find happiness in giving happiness. The school where I presently work is responsible for collecting food and money to give out as many as 200 baskets at Thanksgiving. It is always a joyous occasion on the day the students stream from every room to load the baskets on the truck for distribution. One Christmas I accompanied my husband to distribute Christmas baskets to needy families. At first, I was reluctant because I was afraid we might embarrass the recipients, but I was set at ease at

the first house when a child with a look of utter joy reached for a toy. Watching children look through groceries with excitement gave me happiness. At the end of the journey, I felt rewarded.

When I conveyed these thoughts to my husband, he shared his own experience. He was remembering a Christmas from the past. His mother had died, and his father was struggling to keep his family of five children together. Christmas came and there was no money for gifts. That Christmas morning, some people from the community came with food and toys. His gift was a little red toy truck. With much gratitude, he expressed to me his pleasure in receiving the red truck. Don has had many Christmas seasons since that very skimpy one, but he never forgot the one in which someone remembered a motherless four-year-old boy by giving a little red truck. The remembered happiness greatly overshadowed the bleakness of their situation at that time.

Our school is fortunate in that we have a very giving principal. The following story is an excerpt from "The Orange Peal," the newsletter for the employees of Orange County Public Schools.

> Caren, who is a media clerk at Little River Elementary, has a daughter named Traci, who was a senior at University [High School] last year. Traci was unable to attend her graduation ceremony in May, however, because she was hospitalized. When Anna [the principal] learned of Traci's condition, she arranged with her parents to stage a "mini-graduation ceremony" just for Traci. After University's commencement exercises were completed, Anna went to the hospital. She was dressed in her cap and gown and presented Traci with her diploma. Caren said that her daughter was overwhelmed by Anna's kind deed.

This story sounds small-townish, but University High School has over 4,300 students enrolled. Yes, Anna Diaz expended a lot of energy to drive across town to visit a hospital after sitting through a lengthy graduation ceremony, but her actions brought happiness to a small group that will never forget her. As a result of her thoughtfulness and sacrifice, she also reaped self-satisfaction.

Our school student newspaper, *The Torch,* offered space for guest writers. One student took the opportunity to thank one of her teachers from the previous year for an incredible turn-around in her life. The class was English I and the teacher was Julia Gollhofer, a second-year teacher. Crystal Kellogg wrote

> An English teacher, Julia Gollhofer, made me reach for new goals that I achieved and do things I never thought capable. She pushed me to do my best all the time and put new ideas in front of me, in which I could participate . . . Ms. Gollhofer informed me of extra credit I could do and community service I could be involved in . . . .
>
> So, I started doing extra credit projects, and that led me to actually caring about my grades. . . . Ms. Gollhofer helped me get some hours of community service and I found out that I liked helping people, so I got in touch with a local alternative living center. Volunteering made me realize that I was making people happy and that made me happy and my grades started going up. I started to like school and now a year and a half later, I love going to school and learning new things. Now I

am making straight A's and I have a better outlook on life. So to all who believe they are doing their best, but just can't make A's, look at me—I went from hating school and making D's and F's, to now making straight A's.

The real hero here is Julia Gollhofer, but she is not unlike the many others throughout the hallways who give encouragement and motivation to struggling students. The student becomes the product of many layers of instruction, inspiration, and care that is administered year after year. The extra effort given by the teacher may never be documented, but the successful student is the reward.

I heard about a town in Florida that wanted to cover up a garbage dump with a shopping center. It took a lot of effort to cover over the garbage and lots of asphalt to conceal all evidence that the beautiful mall had once been the dump. There are students who come to us with years of garbage, and we as teachers cannot possibly create a makeover in the short time we have with them. However, our semester or year of exposure will definitely add a layer of influence to the lives of those students. It's like laminating wood. Many flat strips are glued together to make a strong beam for building. We are just one of the strips in the beam, but our input counts.

The young interns who come to our school fascinate me. I wonder what their stories are. Why did they choose teaching? What are their goals, expectations, dreams? Occasionally, I will spend some time chatting with an intern. This fall, a young man shared this story. He said the students had asked him why he had chosen to become a teacher since the position does not pay much money, and he answered the students in this manner:

> An old man was on the end of a dock spending his day fishing. A young tycoon comes along and asks, "What are you going to do with the fish you catch?" The elderly man answered, "I will take them home and fry them for supper."
>
> The tycoon suggested, "If you will take these fish to market, then you could buy a cast net, and tomorrow your catch could be twice as many." The old man replied, "Why would I want to do that?"
>
> The tycoon enthusiastically went on, "You can take all the fish that you catch for many days to the market, and eventually you could buy a boat." The old man replied, "Why would I want to do that?" Seeing the opportunities, the tycoon continued, "Your earning would increase as you filled the boat with fish to sell. Why, man, eventually you could even add more boats and have your own fishing fleet." To this, the old man replied, "Why would I want to do that?" The tycoon's final and triumphal answer was the plum, "Then you could retire and do what you want." The old man replied, "I'm doing that now."

The young intern, who shared with me the story, gave a broad smile at the end and said, "So, that is what I tell the students who ask me about my career choice. There are always options and opportunities, but teaching is what I want to do and what I do well."

A former coworker constantly complained of the unfairness of life. He always got the worst classroom, the worst schedule, the worst duty, the worst students, the worst interfering parents, the most unfair evaluations . . . the list was endless. He was very creative in his language to describe what "life" was doing to him. He began his graduate program, and I naively thought that he would find happiness in his new goals. But, no! The university was out to mess over his program. He had scheduling difficulties, poor class choices, stupid professors, insane assignments, and his program counselor must have fallen off a truck that happened to be passing by the University of Central Florida. Was I surprised when he announced he was relocating? He expected happiness to ride on other people's actions. By putting others in charge of his happiness, he denied himself the right to choose. He became a critic rather than a decider. It was easy to yield to the temptation of feeling shortchanged.

The day I quit complaining about my job was the day I was told that I was included in the Florida budget cuts. After a month of uncertainty and some job hunting, I was rehired; but I was cured of complaining. Students had never been more beautiful, papers were easier to grade, and lesson plans were created and submitted with happy thoughts. Getting out of bed at 5:30 a.m. even became easier. Complaining can become a thoughtless habit. We can use complaints for just something to say, failing to realize that the listener may interpret them seriously and that our complaints can create a negative atmosphere in and out of the classroom.

One way in which to solve a problem is to find out what doesn't work. To just accept unhappiness without any attempt to alleviate the pain is similar to accepting a headache with unused pain relievers close by. It may sound negative, but we need to learn what makes us unhappy before we can be happy. The body has an amazing denial system. When we gather our evidence and make the diagnosis, we must take action. Consulting a doctor for the cure of an illness is useless unless we carry through with the prescription for the remedy. We may never be canonized as a saint, but we can make life more pleasant for ourselves and for others with whom we associate by raising our level of happiness.